TELL ME WHY

ANSWERING TOUGH QUESTIONS ABOUT THE FAITH

RONDA DE SOLA CHERVIN
MSGR. JOSEPH POLLARD

Our Sunday Visitor Publishing Division
Our Sunday Visitor, Inc.
Huntington, Indiana 46750

Cover design by Rebecca J. Heaston

PRINTED IN THE UNITED STATES OF AMERICA

CONTENTS

Foreword

I am pleased to pen this foreword to the book *Tell Me Why*. The book is the work of two professors at St. John's Seminary, one in the field of philosophy and the other in theology. It reflects both the rigorous approach of trained minds and a deep sense of personal fulfillment and joy in Jesus and the Church.

In the years prior to the great Second Vatican Council, Pope John XXIII was much saddened by a world in which so many people lived under officially atheistic governments or in a freely imposed lifestyle devoid of God's influence. He summoned the council in great part to address this widespread phenomenon. In consequence, the Church is called to evangelization — to the presentation of the Lord's call to grace to modern men and women.

It is this spirit and energy that imbue the authors' labor of love that is this book. I applaud the wonderful gifts and talents of Monsignor Joseph Pollard and Ronda Chervin, Ph.D., who have not only taught our seminarians so effectively over the years but have also inspired them with the depth of their own faith-lives and the deep commitment of their discipleship with Jesus Christ. They have brought to our seminarians far more than education, and I know that all who use this book will be lifted up in spirit to see the face of Jesus and to follow his ways ever more closely.

The book is based on a very popular elective course the authors have offered our future priests. The list of questions such a course and book might deal with could be almost endless. But they have chosen a core group of topics close to the mind and heart of the seeker of truth today.

I hope that many good people struggling for meaning and purpose in the anonymity of society today will find this book useful, and that our religious educators, students, and all in Church leadership roles will use the work to help them be instruments of the Lord in achieving the purpose of his life: "I have come so that [you] may have life and have it to the full" (John 10:10, *Jerusalem Bible*).

CARDINAL ROGER MAHONY
ARCHBISHOP OF LOS ANGELES

Introduction

Fervent Catholics are surprised that everyone in the whole world is not finding joy in being part of our Church. Most non-Catholics, on the other hand, are surprised that anyone is part of that Church.

"Tell me why I should be a Catholic when . . ." is the beginning of a list of questions that might seem endless, such as "Tell me why I should be a Catholic when some Catholic teachings are not Bible-based?" Some of these queries come from those who do not believe in a personal God at all. Others come from people who love God but dislike all institutional churches. Amazement and even scorn can come from members of other religions who consider the Catholic Church to be the most evil.

And how about former Catholics? They might wonder why anyone stays in a church they find so boring, dead, or cruel. Even practicing Catholics have lots of questions or nagging doubts.

This book is designed to respond to some of these questions. It is written by two Catholics of quite different backgrounds. One of them, Msgr. Joseph Pollard, was baptized as a baby in Ireland among family and friends who had loved the Catholic Church for generations. Monsignor Pollard — a professor of theology at St. John's Seminary in Camarillo, California — is the author of many popular books and articles about the Catholic faith, with many years of experience in reaching out to non-Catholics as a pastor. The other author, Dr. Ronda Chervin, was baptized as a Catholic at the age of twenty-one in 1959, having come from a mostly Jewish but atheistic family. She is a professor of philosophy at St. John's Seminary, a wife and mother, author of numerous books and articles for the laity about faith and everyday life, and an international lecturer.

It is the authors' prayer that this book will be of use to many: to readers who dislike the Church intensely but have been persuaded to just read one book; to those intrigued by the Church but are quite doubtful of her claims; to Catholic parishioners who wonder if they are in the right Church; to pastors and their teams working in classes with non-Catholic adults; and to those in Catholic youth ministry, high-school religion classes, adult education, and home-study programs.

TELL ME WHY I SHOULD BE A CATHOLIC WHEN . . .

the gods of the New Age are more exciting?

When we try to interest friends of ours in the Catholic faith, the question they ask is this: Tell me why I should be a Catholic when I can explore so many interesting spiritual paths on my own?

Very often such seekers are highly spiritual in the sense of being eager to live in categories higher than those offered by our materialistically minded society. They are fascinated by the exotic symbols and rites of other religions. Some of them have tried out some Asian religions in their American forms. Such persons may also sometimes attend Catholic services (midnight Mass on Christmas Eve, for instance) or go to a Jewish Seder on Passover with other friends.

Many spiritual explorers are happy to make contact with certain elements of Catholic tradition they find beautiful such as Gregorian chant or stained-glass windows. Yet some show little interest in finding out what led the composers and artists to such fervor.

Usually sharing with such friends reveals a resistance to the idea of what Catholics would call a personal God. The notion of a personal God is often associated with images of God as an old man with a beard. Instead, many New Agers think of God more in terms of an impersonal transcendent energy — a force perhaps identified with the sort of feeling of radiance we all have sometimes when looking at something as beautiful as an ocean or a view from a mountaintop.

By contrast, the way Catholics talk about religion can seem narrow. In fact, we agree that there are Catholics who can seem so focused on specific practices of their religion (such as going to Sunday liturgy or praying the Rosary) that they give the impression that other spiritualities don't even exist, except perhaps as a temptation. Sometimes the way Catholics act can give the impression of a concentration on their own salvation with ignorance of all other religious traditions. Or a non-Catholic looking at a work of art such as Michelangelo's creation showing God the Father in human form extending his finger toward Adam to give him life may get the false idea that Catholics think God is bodily.

What we really believe is that God is pure spirit — completely immaterial, beyond weight and measure — that is, being.

Yet Catholics do not think of God either as simply an impersonal divine energy. God revealed himself to the people of the Old Testament as a personal God: "I am who I am." "Personal" means consciously aware, able to think, able to love. These attributes do not require a physical body. "Human beings" are embodied persons. Jesus, the Son of God, was incarnate in the flesh. But God himself is pure personal being without any physical dimension.

When you think about it, wouldn't it be strange to think a being *greater* than us, great enough to create the whole world, wouldn't also have the greatness of consciousness? Could God be less than us because we picture him as *unconscious* — a mere force or energy?

The first step, then, to beginning to understand the Catholic religion is to realize that a personal God is the center of it all.

But how do we know, a seeker might ask, that such a personal God even exists? Scripture tells us that we can come to some conviction about such a God just by looking around us: "For from the greatness and beauty of created things comes a corresponding perception of their Creator" (Wisdom 13:5).

Catholic tradition speaks to us of the God of Scripture. Catholic tradition also includes formal demonstrations of the existence of this Creator-God. Here are some of these proofs. At the end of each one, reflections from contemporary scientists will be given to show that it is not true, as we so imagine, that no scientist could believe in a Creator-God.

The Causal Argument

The causal argument of St. Thomas Aquinas[1] can be briefly and informally stated in this manner: "All around us we see an orderly world with one after another of visible effects springing from previous causes. Nothing just happens for no reason whatsoever. What seven-year-old can convince his mother that the milk spilled all over the kitchen floor because it just happened to go there without any cause?"

Nothing can just cause itself, because it would have to exist prior to itself, which is a contradiction.

You may think, "Well, causes might go back and continue to do so infinitely with no beginning." To this Aquinas argued that such an imaginary backward look explains nothing. Unless there is one first cause, which we call God, nothing can take place, for each of the subsequent causes depends on some original cause to start the whole train of causality going.

You might ask now: "If everything has to have a cause, who caused God?" The basic answer Aquinas would give is simple, though you might need to study lots of philosophy to understand it perfectly. The types of beings that need causes are of the kind that are destructible, that come to be and pass away. God is by definition an *absolute* being. He has no beginning or end, so he doesn't need a cause.

Yet you might respond, "Maybe it's not God but the whole cosmos that is absolute." Could that be true?

Contemporary scientists think that there must have been a beginning to time, not for philosophical reasons but for scientific ones. The so-called big bang theory holds that time had an absolute beginning fifteen to twenty billion years ago.

Specifically, the astronomer Robert Jastrow reports that there is evidence that the universe came into existence abruptly and that this description corresponds to the biblical view: "The evidence lies in the fact that all the galaxies — the great clusters of stars that populate the heavens — are moving away from us and one another at enormous speeds, as if they were recoiling from the scene of a great explosion. If the motions of the outward-moving galaxies are traced backwards in time, we find that they all come together, so to speak, about 20 billion years ago. At that time all the matter in the Universe was packed into one dense mass under enormous pressure, and with temperatures ranging up to trillions of degrees. The picture suggests the explosion of a cosmic hydrogen bomb. The instant in which the cosmic bomb exploded marked the birth of the universe."[2]

Here is another demonstration from the writings of Thomas Aquinas:

The Argument From Contingency

Summarized, Thomas thought that everything we know in nature is only possible (contingent) — that is, it happens to exist, but it might never have existed. If your parents did not happen to meet and mate at exactly the date of your conception, you would not exist. This makes you *contingent*, or dependent, rather than being an absolute, totally independent being. There could have been a world with no trees, or one with no TV.

If there was no God to create time, then there must be an infinite amount of time. But within an infinite amount of time there would have to have been a world not only where there were no trees or TV but also a world when nothing at all existed.

However, if there were ever a time when nothing existed, nothing could exist now, for you cannot get anything out of nothing. Therefore, for anything at all to exist, there must be something in existence that was always there by reason of its own necessity, an absolute being: God.

Stanley L. Jaki in an article entitled "From Scientific Cosmology to a Created Universe"[3] argues that Einstein's theories really lead away from the idea of an infinite universe as a reason *not* to need a God. Instead, they lead us toward the image of a specific universe. This specificity, Jaki theorizes, signifies contingency, or dependence, on something else!

A book called *The New Story of Science* [4] advances the claim that the old science tended to deny a Creator-God, but the new story of science is more positive: "In the new story of science (post-mechanistic) the whole universe, including matter, energy, space and time, is a one-time event and had a definite beginning. But something must have always existed; for if ever absolutely nothing existed, then nothing would exist now, since nothing comes from nothing. The material universe cannot be the thing that always existed because matter had a beginning . . . this means that what has always existed is non-material. The only non-material reality seems to be mind. If mind is what has always existed, then matter must have been brought into existence by a mind that always was."[5]

Still, someone might object, perhaps everything came to be not because of a Creator-God but by chance. This objection, which can seem so clear-cut, rests on a tremendous misunderstanding. It makes it seem as if "chance" is an actual being, or entity, whereas chance is really not a being at all but a name for lack of knowledge about causes. When I say, "I met John by chance at the shopping mall," I don't mean that there is a being called *chance* who pushed John to come to the mall, but rather that he came for reasons I would not have predicted. Chance is not an agent, like a transmitter. And it is certainly not a source of being that could create a universe!

Yet another popular way of understanding why there is a Creator-God is called:

The Argument From Purpose and Design

In summary, all around us we see order and purpose in nature. To use an example most of us would consider fairly awesome, take the human eye, so intricately ordered in its myriad parts that it makes it possible for many creatures to be able to see. Can order such as this come about by coincidence?

If you found a watch in the middle of the desert, would you think the sand simply formed such a mechanism, or would you think that it was designed by an intelligent being for a purpose? A watch is made by a human intelligence. But since eyes do not consciously plan themselves to be able to see, any more than an arrow by itself aims at a target, it is plain that all these unconscious beings such as eyes and horns, or ears and skin, must be designed and governed by an intelligent being, and this being we call God.

Some think that evolutionary theory has rendered the argument from design to be outmoded. Things develop, it is argued, not by design but by the survival of the fittest, as Darwin believed. Creatures who happened to have eyes survived better, and that is why we see many around us with eyes on their faces.

It is surprising to learn that such counterarguments have been answered not only by religious philosophers but by scientists themselves. In an article entitled "Science and the Divine Origin of Life,"[6] Professor Chandra Wickramasinghe claims that his research in the area of the biochemistry of life contradicts the old evolutionary theory.

He tells us: "All the conditions were wrong for life to start on the earth. The atmosphere of the earth was supposed to be of a character that permitted the formation of complex organic materials, according to the conventional (evolutionary) story, and our investigation revealed to us that the earth's atmosphere could not have had this character. In technical language, a necessary requirement for organic soups to form on the earth is that the early earth's atmosphere had to be reducing, that is to say it had to have a deficit of oxygen, of free oxygen atoms . . . the earth's atmosphere was never of the right character to form this organic soup."[7]

Wickramasinghe thinks that such improbabilities indicate the need for a God who planned for life to be able to flourish in his world, in spite of all the ways it would not evolve naturally.

A biochemist named Sheldrake, quoted in the same volume,[8] claims that there is no more probability of the world evolving from chance out of some original matter than that all the letters in a Scrabble game laid out in the wind would eventually form the sonnets of Shakespeare!

* * *

It seems to people of all faiths — Catholics, Jews, Protestants, and Muslims — that the sort of ideas presented above are at least sufficiently reasonable to convince a genuine seeker to consider trying to find out more about a personal Creator-God.

Perhaps you are such a person. Maybe you are blocked from getting closer to a personal God by an identification of the traditional God with guilt feelings. Consider, however, that the God Christians believe in is one whose merciful love is so great that the believer does not live in dread but in hope and joy, knowing God can forgive any sin past or present if repented of.

In the course of the following chapters, more perspectives will be given for you to evaluate yourself about the way God has chosen to interact with the human beings he created.

This chapter will end with a sketch about a man who found the personal Creator-God after years of seeking:

Many centuries ago there was a man who could not find a satisfying religious outlook. He had been brought up by a Catholic mother, but he ridiculed her faith as superstitious and narrow. His name was Augustine and he grew up in Egypt in the fourth century A.D.

Although brilliant and searching, Augustine's personal life even as a youth was far from morally stable. He hung around with a thieving gang of youths and he indulged in sexual pleasure freely.

A student of rhetoric — the rules of speechmaking — Augustine became himself, as a young adult, a teacher of this art. In his spare time he joined with a group of friends in trying out whatever was being offered in the way of spiritual enlightenment. The chief group to attract him was called the Manichees. This sect was interested in gods of light and darkness. Later on, discouraged by the failure of the greatest wise man of the group to answer his questions, Augustine studied the philosophers. They helped him to grasp the idea of immateriality — that there could be spiritual beings rather than all things being types of matter or what we would call energy.

Eventually Augustine underwent a tremendous dramatic conversion to the Person of Jesus Christ in his Church. Far from feeling trapped, his vision expanded infinitely. In the description of his conversion to be found in *The Confessions of St. Augustine* he wrote: "And Thee would man praise; man, but a particle of Thy creation, that bears about him his mortality . . . for Thou madest us for Thyself and restless are our hearts until they rest in Thee."

The radiant joy that he found in the personal God of Scripture was to overflow in such a manner as to convert many of his friends. So unable was he to contain this rapture that his mother had to upbraid him for shocking all and sundry by singing hymns aloud even in the outhouse! Eventually he became a priest and bishop and one of the greatest writers of all times.

The reading of Augustine's *Confessions*, needless to say, has been a turning point for many a fervent seeker after spiritual truth.

ENDNOTES

1. The arguments for God's existence to follow can be found in more detail in the *Summa Theologica*, Parts 1, 2. For easy-to-read excerpts from the *Summa Theologica* as well as explanatory footnotes see Peter Kreeft, *Summa of the Summa* (San Francisco: Ignatius Press, 1990).
2. See *The Intellectuals Speak Out About God*, ed. by Roy Abraham Varghese (Chicago: Regnery, 1984), p. 15.
3. Ibid., pp. 61-78.
4. Robert M. Augros and George N. Stanciu, *The New Story of Science* (Chicago: Regnery, 1984).

5. Ibid., pp. 63-64.
6. *The Intellectuals Speak Out About God*, pp. 23-37.
7. Ibid., pp. 24-25.
8. Ibid., pp. 51-59.

TELL ME WHY I SHOULD BE A CATHOLIC WHEN...

I can make up my own religion and go to God alone?

Even among those who accept a personal God, there are some who say, "I don't need the Church: I can go to God alone." I first heard this statement from a high-school senior when I was directing a retreat for public high-school students. I've heard it since from adults and teens in different forms. "There's too much religion and too little real worship of God." "History is full of churches fighting one another and ignoring God." "I can relate to God in my own heart more honestly than by using some church's rules and dogmas." A man once said to me: "I don't find God in any church: I find him in my own heart." These statements ask, in effect, the question, "Why the Church at all?"

The ultimate answer to this question has to go back to Christ himself. For the Church is "born from the heart of Christ"[1] whose authority and divinity we consider in Chapter 4. If you believe that there is no need or reason for a formal church structure, kindly read on.

I, too, have felt the temptation of dispensing with religion and churches and Holy Scriptures and popes and bishops and clergy and regulations — and getting to a place in my life where there is just "God and me" without all this intervening super-structure. I've felt like saying, "Get out of the way:

you just block the free access that ought to obtain between my loving God and me!" I remember a scene in a TV film about immigrants to America in which one immigrant tells the other, while en route by ship, what America means to him. It is freedom, he explains. And then, without being asked, he defines freedom. It is to live in a country where he will not have to bow down to the king and the local lord, the sheriff and the bailiff, the tax collector and the army recruiter, the archbishop and the bishop, the pastor and the curate, and the Church that seems to assign one to hell or to heaven.

I can resonate with that man. There is much that is not only emotionally true in his story but religiously true as well. If, indeed, God had chosen to do so he could have arranged that each of us should relate with him directly, without the need of formal religions or churches; and in such an arrangement each of us would *have* to go to God alone and directly and without external structures or help of similar kind. In fact, today as throughout human history, there are individual persons who relate with God in such a way and who, I am sure, are most loved of God and pleasing to him. But we *do* need the Church, and we really should not have to make up our own religion, and I can confidently say that it just isn't God's will that we should "go it alone." God did not make us "loners." He made us social beings. I do not bring myself into this world alone. I cannot live by myself in this life alone. Heaven does not exist just for God and me alone. I recall the profound line of John Donne: "No man is an island, entire of itself."

If God had chosen the "alone" way for me to relate

with him, then that would be the normal, the only, and the correct way to go to him. I would *have* to form my own religion. But God has chosen another way and a much better way. It is the way *he* (not I) has stipulated for all of his children.

We see this stipulation (or intention) of God in the very nature of religion. Religion results from human beings' awareness of the supernatural and the transcendent. The study of the human psychology of religion and of the forms of religion that this psychology has expressed in history teaches us a number of things, the most important being that in order to prevent religion from "dissolving into a haze of private satisfaction"[2] it has taken on external concrete forms that always involve others. The Church is one such external concrete form.

God chose to form Judaism under the old covenant in order to prepare the way for the Redeemer who would undo the sin of Adam and restore us to God's friendship. God fashioned Israel as his special people. He spoke to them through the *mediation* of revelation and prophecy. The words of the prophets shaped them into a holy people, God's people. God did not leave each person alone to hammer out his or her individual way to him. (The Bible shows how quickly Adam strayed from God when left to his own individual groping.) The Old Testament displays a whole people at worship, formed and fed on the word of God.

Then comes Jesus. St. Paul writes: "Long ago, God spoke to our ancestors in many and various ways by the prophets, but in these last days he has spoken to us by a Son. . ." (Hebrews 1:1-2). Jesus, like God, his Father, also fashions a people around him. His redemption of us and our salvation does not come to each of us as individuals but as members of a believing community, the Church. Jesus chose others to help him in this work. Right from the beginning of his public ministry, Jesus is assisted by the apostles and the disciples. He forms a community and instructs this community. Later, he sends this community into the world to continue to *mediate* his message and his saving grace. At times, this community is called "our company" during the Lord's historical life, or "the church" after his ascension (for example, note the many greetings of Paul and John "to the Church which is at Ephesus" — or at Rome, or at Jerusalem, etc.).

One cannot bypass the fact that God conducted the old covenant through the mediation of the people of Israel and that the new covenant is conducted through the mediation of the Church. For any of us to try to "go it alone" or to "bypass the Church" is to engage in a form of individualism and privatization that ignores the express will of God in the matter of how he wishes to relate with each of us and save us. Word, will of God, and saving grace are *mediated* through the Church by God's will and loving disposition. Who am I to attempt to ignore that plan?

Some who have difficulty living the community (that is, the social) nature of the Church may well have had negative experiences with family and with authority figures when growing up. But this difficulty *can* be eliminated in the parish or Church group where authority is a loving service and greatness is "love of the brethren."

As I look back on my life I realize that all I have of

Scripture and grace was given to me by others — by the Church. I have generated nothing of saving word and saving grace on my own. I cannot — alone — even fulfill the last will and testament of Jesus in my own regard. "Then he took a loaf of bread, and . . . broke it and gave it to them [his disciples], saying, 'This is my body, which is given for you. Do this in remembrance of me' " (Luke 22:19). I cannot receive this Eucharist without the Church. I cannot find it alone, in my room, on the beach, on the mountain-top, in a book, or by personal prayer. And yet Jesus said: "Very truly, I tell you, unless you eat the flesh of the Son of Man and drink his blood, you have no life in you. Those who eat my flesh and drink my blood have eternal life, and I will raise them up on the last day" (John 6:53-54). This is the Eucharist (called "the breaking of the bread"), which dominates the Acts of the Apostles, often called the history book of the earliest days of Christianity.

Similarly, Jesus told Nicodemus that "no one can enter the kingdom of God without being born of water and Spirit" (John 3:5). But in every New Testament instance, such a baptism cannot be given to oneself by oneself. It is given one through the mediation of another, through the Church. Jesus did not establish a church or a kingdom for each believer but a church and a kingdom of the many believers united in faith and love and grace together. For Jesus came from a family of Persons, the Trinity. He did not come on his own: he was sent by Others. The very meaning of "church" is: the assembly, the gathering, the congregation, the community. Religion is a communitarian venture established by Jesus. It is the agency for mediating the salvation and grace of Jesus now. It is the very opposite of man's attempt to "go it alone" or to "do it my way" instead of God's way.

If I say that I do not need the Church, that I can go to God alone, I am asserting, in effect, that God's revealed way of dealing with us for the past two thousand years is not good enough for me. I am saying that the incarnation of the Son of God — and its forms of mediation between God and me — is not necessary for me. I put myself outside the old and the new covenants, the Judaic and the Christian experiences of the God who reveals himself as a community of Persons in relationship with a human community of faith.

Two aspects of the Church have influenced me greatly since my youth. Both are found in the Scriptures. St. Paul writes of the Church as Christ's bride in the fifth chapter of his letter to the Ephesians. Jesus is the bridegroom and the Church is his beloved bride. Consequently, I have always seen the sins of the Church as the aberrations of individual members of the Church and I have been conscious of how my own sins are responsible for the "spots" and "wrinkles" of which St. Paul speaks. I do not confuse the beauty of the Church (as the Lord's beloved) with the disfigurements that unworthy believers have burdened the bride with throughout history and even today. All the more am I thereby committed to Christ's bride, trying in my poor way to protect her beauty and uphold her marriage with the Lord. (For more on the history of sin in the Church, see Chapter 5 of this work.)

The second scriptural passage is a dramatic one. Jesus says of the authority of the Church: "He who listens to you listens to me" and "He who will not listen to the Church, let him be to you anathema [that is, a castaway]" (paraphrase of Matthew 18:15, 17). Despite the Lord's remarkable identification here of the Church with himself, many seekers — and even some believers — find it difficult to accept the Church's light and guidance. There is a submission of the intellect and the will required here that we all find difficult to offer — and yet there is a great freedom. One does not really submit in a craven way but in a liberative way; for the seeker of saving truth is as the seeker in any area of human questing — liberated and enhanced by finding the truth.

But instead of finding *one* version of the truth, thinking people are confused and scandalized by the multiplicity of versions of Christianity that exists today. In times past, this was often described as acceptable varieties of the truth of Jesus or as a healthy pluralism (as though one were dealing with just cultural and ethnic expressions of the one truth). But the confusion and the scandal have arisen because men and women, down through the centuries, have torn the unity of Christ's truth and Church asunder. Today, in the United States alone, there are some fifteen hundred versions of the *one* truth and Church of Jesus (that is, confessional churches). If they were united on all important teachings and on the instruments of grace, then the multiplicity might be explained in some intelligent manner. But that is not the case. There is chaotic divergence even on fundamentals. The Bible is forced to yield as many interpretations of God's word as each one's fancy chooses, and the Holy Spirit is offered as speaking each one's *contradictory* truth. In such an arena, Jesus' indivisible word is divisible in the extreme, and the Spirit of truth and unity given by Jesus to his bride is manifested as a Spirit of contradiction and chaos.

How does one avoid such a lamentable state for oneself? One must cast one's faith with the Church as she came into being with Jesus, the Church of the apostolic age, the Church grounded on Peter to whom the Lord gave "the keys of the kingdom of heaven" (see Matthew 16:19). It is not enough to simply reach back into history and take hold of some truths of the early days. For the Church is not just a collection of truths. She is a living tradition, the bride forever, the assigned teacher, the one on whom the Lord sent his Spirit that first Pentecost, and the one that is directed by that indivisible Spirit until the Lord comes again and which cannot teach error, confusion, or contradiction. I need the Church for authentic teaching and I need her for sacramental saving grace. I do not need a version that is "reformed" by men in rebellion with the living tradition that has never lost (because it could never lose) the presence of the given Spirit of truth. Any church emerging in history as someone's "reformed" version of *the* Church is historically too late to be the Lord's bride, and such a "church" is theologically presumptive in choosing to ignore that the Spirit, which cannot err, was given definitively to the Church of the definitive Pentecost long ago.

In many ways, the seeker who tries to "go it alone" is companion to the reformers and originators of churches in history. They, too, have tried in a sense to "do it their way," to remake the Church — as one critic wrote — according to their own image and

27

likeness as if Jesus had not done the original planning well and as though the Holy Spirit had fallen asleep on the job during most of the historical life of the Church.

The journey of so many converts to the Catholic Church seems to reflect that same twofold issue: "Is it God's will that I relate with him 'alone' and without benefit of the Church; and if I can't, how do I find the Church that is the Lord's bride?" Their journeys are much as I have journeyed in these pages. They found that they simply could no longer go to God alone with any real assurance, and then they journeyed through history to find the true bride of Christ, the Church of the apostles and the Fathers.

As a student, I remember listening on BBC radio to the British poet Dame Edith Sitwell explaining to the interviewer how her search for an authentic relationship with God merely led her into a philosophical morass. She rejected "easy" salvation and "cheap" grace because she knew that these were not to be found in the original Church of the early Christian centuries. She realized, she said, that she needed "the fire, the discipline, and the authority" of that original Church. She found what she was seeking in Catholicism.

The same kind of practical and authentic relationship with the Lord was at back of G. K. Chesterton's conversion to the Church in the generation prior to Sitwell. He did not see the Church as a historical event of the past but a living form in the present. Brilliant though he was, Chesterton also had gone the route of "going it alone." In the last chapter of *Orthodoxy*, he writes: "The Christian Church in its practical relation to my soul is a living teacher, not a dead one."[3]

For him, the philosophies of men are dead. His own brilliance cannot save him. But the Catholic Church is alive with God's word, with the sacraments of saving grace, and with the living presence of the Lord.

But the most persuasive reason why the Church should not be bypassed by the seeker of God remains the identification that Jesus himself made between the Church and himself (as noted already in the reference to Matthew 18:17). It is repeated, dramatically, in the greatest conversion story of all — the transformation of the anti-Church zealot, Saul of Tarsus, into the magnificent Church missionary, St. Paul. The story (Acts 9:1-9) is so simple that one almost misses the effortlessness with which Jesus identifies the Church as interchangeable with himself:

> Meanwhile Saul, still breathing threats and murder against the disciples of the Lord, went to the high priest and asked him for letters to the synagogues at Damascus so that if he found any who belonged to the Way [that is, Christianity], men or women, he might bring them bound to Jerusalem. Now as he was going along and approaching Damascus, suddenly a light from heaven flashed around him. He fell to the ground and heard a voice saying to him, "Saul, Saul, why do you persecute me?" He asked, "Who are you, Lord?" The reply came, "I am Jesus, whom you are persecuting. But get up and enter the city, and you will be told what you are to do." The men who were traveling with him stood

speechless because they heard the voice but saw no one. Saul got up from the ground, and though his eyes were open, he could see nothing; so they led him by the hand and brought him into Damascus. For three days he was without sight, and neither ate nor drank.

ENDNOTES

1. An allusion to Genesis 2:21-22, in which Eve is fashioned from a rib taken from Adam's side.
2. Karl Rahner and Herbert Vorgrimler, *Theological Dictionary* (New York: Seabury Press, 1973), p. 400.
3. G. K. Chesterton, *Orthodoxy* (London: The Bodley Head, 1949), p. 266.

TELL ME WHY I SHOULD BE A CATHOLIC WHEN...

there is so much pain in the world it seems there cannot be a God of love?

The greatest cause of doubt about the Catholic philosophy of life is the reality of suffering in this world. How could a good, loving God allow so much pain when he could stop it immediately by means of his miraculous powers?

High on the list of such baffling sufferings are these:

● The death of infants.

● The destruction of whole communities in earthquakes, floods, drought, and famine as well as painful, lingering death caused by illness.

● A food chain that depends on each species devouring another species to survive.

Some suffering — such as that resulting from war, murder, abortion, incest, rape, abandonment, infidelity, theft, drug and alcohol abuse — is clearly caused not by God but by mankind. A great portion of human suffering is caused by people (against whom we lock our doors and bar our windows at night) — certainly not God!

When we reflect on these evils, however, we tend to feel that there was a moment when God could have but did not intervene! "If only my child had left home two minutes earlier (stopped by God), she would not have crossed the path of that rapist!" "If I hadn't lost my good job (God could have changed the boss's mind), we wouldn't be living in the bad neighborhood where my son joined the gang that got him into drugs." "If I had gotten pregnant three months later I would have met Joe and we would have gotten married and kept the baby."

The basic dilemma is this: if God is loving and good he would have made his creatures happy, for God is by definition almighty, and an all-powerful God can do anything. But so many people are unhappy. Therefore, God lacks either goodness or total power (as Woody Allen jests: maybe God isn't evil, he's just an underachiever).

Actually, to get down to it, it is hard to understand why God created human beings at all. It is easy to picture a world of oceans, mountains, plants, animals, all just there flourishing but not needing to cause any pain — the world we usually imagine Eden was. It is when we add free-will characters such as angels and humans that the problem begins. It is the bad angel, Satan, who tempts man to explore disobedience and evil, and Adam and Eve who take him up on it. From that flow all the evils we listed earlier.

So why did God create persons who can disobey him? Why did God create anything at all, for that matter, since he was happy in his goodness with just the Trinity for company?

Religious philosophers have racked their brains over that one for many centuries. One of the best answers to be found is in the writings of Thomas Aquinas: goodness is naturally diffusive. What does that mean? It is the very nature of something good either to overflow or to create. For Jews and Christians, Scripture is our source of truth. The Bible tells us not that God overflowed but that he created.

An analogy might help. Why is it that usually at the very peak of love between two people, when they feel most full, they start thinking of starting a family? Then after two children if not sooner, full of delight, they start thinking about a house, and maybe pets, and maybe more children. In fact, the greater their happiness, the more they want to create! Maybe God is like us that way. Maybe he is so delighted with his creation that he planned for it always to grow.

Scripture tells us that angels and humans are the most like God because they are *conscious intelligent beings who can know and will and love as God can*. But, given the fact that angels and humans can disobey God and cause endless evils, shouldn't God have trashed the idea of creating them? Well, consider the fact that when you dream of a child of your own you know that this child will probably sin and also be the victim of sin. This thought causes some people never to procreate, but most believe it is worth it. Somehow they hope that the good in life and the good they hope for in an afterlife will make up for all the pain. Maybe God thinks that way, too. It seems so!

Such reflections may provide insight, but they never totally satisfy the human mind, especially when one is confronted with severe pain or when one sees loved ones suffering. In fact, suffering remains a mystery in the sense of never being resolved on this earth.

But being a mystery does not mean that no light

can be shed on it. The result of deeper and deeper thought is not so much to be convinced that there is no problem as to become convinced that it is right to love God, believing him to be good, even though it is not clear why everything happens as it does with such painful results.

Among the most convincing insights to be found in contemporary religious literature concerning the problem of how a good God could allow so much suffering in the world is the book *The Problem of Pain* by C. S. Lewis.

Starting with the dilemma as stated above — namely that since God is almighty and supposedly good, he must be able to make us happy, so that our pain militates against his existence or at least against his goodness — Lewis finds a solution in a close examination of the key words in this puzzle: almighty, good, and happy.

First, let's look at the concept of all-powerfulness. Many people get confused because they do not understand that to be able to do everything does not mean to be able to do what is self-contradictory. A famous old riddle goes this way: If God can do anything, can he create a square circle? This question is actually absurd, for to be able to create anything doesn't mean to create a nothing. A square circle is really a nothing because it is a contradiction in terms. There cannot be a square circle not because God is limited but because it is an empty word — a nonentity.

Now, according to Lewis, the same analysis can be done with respect to the possibility of God creating a person (angel or human) who is free yet totally controlled by God! Since it is the very nature of a person to be free, a totally controlled person is just not a person.

What does this have to do with the problem of suffering? Well, consider the matter. Huge hunks of pain are caused by free-will decisions of humans, such as murders, thefts, wars, and incest. Now if God simply waved a wand and destroyed the gun of the murderer, the hand of the thief, the bomb of the enemy, the organs of the rapist, how would these people be free?

It appears that given the choice of not creating any persons at all and creating persons whose freedom could hurt others, God chose to create us. Why? Augustine says because God can bring good out of evil. "Really? I don't see it," you might reply. On earth we don't find justice, but in eternity God can make justice reign. There all our tears will be wiped away, promises Jesus. This means that an all-powerful God must allow for the possibility of the sufferings caused by evil persons as long as he wants to create persons at all. Would it even be worthwhile to create only robots run by himself instead? Would you rather have a robot than a friend, a child, a niece?

What about God's goodness? Here Lewis distinguishes between two meanings of good in our own human way of speaking. Sometimes by calling someone good we mean that the person gives us whatever we want. Other times we call good someone who gives us what is best for us even if there is pain involved. We may sometimes wish to think the dentist is an ogre, but we really admit with all the pain that he is good to put up with all our grimaces and shrieks and groans in an effort to help us retain our teeth in good shape. We may sometimes think that a friend who deals drugs is good because the customer wants these toxic drugs and will feel pleasure for a while after getting them, but we really know the drug dealer is evil because he knows the pain that will result.

Now it is clear that God is not good in the wrong sense of being one who gives us everything we want. One witty writer pointed out that if God gave all of us everything we ever wanted there would be no people left since at one time or another most of us wish at least one person would drop dead quickly!

But does God give us what is best? This is what we believe. We believe that he allows us to suffer because he sees that it can purify us! So, who needs that much purification? That is hard for us to see, especially about ourselves. In *The Problem of Pain* Lewis penetratingly explains how much of our unfeeling indifference to others comes from not understanding their pain from within. The more types of suffering we endure, the more likely that we will relate to others with healing empathy.

Pain also weans us from the world. Since our true home is in heaven, it is not good for us to settle down to the temporary or partial joys and pleasures of what is only an inn on the pilgrimage. It is as if a child would only watch TV dogs and never touch a real one. Real dogs might bite, but they are worth it. A kid addicted to TV might need to be forcibly pulled away from the set and persuaded to explore the real world. An adult addicted to the mixed pleasures of this world might need some goad to look upward at unimaginably greater sources of happiness, such as union with God.

Kahlil Gibran writes in the famous book *The Prophet*: "Your pain is the breaking of the shell that encloses your understanding. Even as the stone of the fruit must break, that its heart may stand in the sun, so must you know pain. And could you keep your heart in wonder at the daily miracles of your life, your pain would not seem less wondrous than your joy; and you would accept the seasons of your heart, even as you have always accepted the seasons that pass over your fields. And you would watch with serenity through the winters of your grief."

This brings us to the last word Lewis analyzes: happiness. By happiness some people mean a feeling of contentment, pleasure, absence of pain. Another meaning of "happy" is "joyful and hopeful."

Obviously God does not keep us content in this life on earth. But that does not mean that all is misery. He gives us joy that is not lasting, and hope in everlasting joy for eternity.

Here is a thought exercise you might do to understand this distinction better. Someone invents a miracle drug. Shoot it into your arm and you will never experience pain again. On the other hand, it will numb you in such a way that you cannot make any decisions or carry out any fresh actions. You will just sit in a corner smiling and content for the rest of your life! Would you take it?

At first it might sound good, especially if you are in physical, emotional, or spiritual pain at the moment. But after a while most human beings would rather put up with a mixture of pain and delight coming with freedom, especially if they anticipate a time in the future when all will be not numb pleasure but real delight caused by the presence of beauty, loved friends, and God himself.

In this way we can see that a real God of love does not create robots to avoid the pain that comes with our sin. He gives what is best rather than what is wanted and postpones our happiness, giving glimpses of it through occasional joys. Consider the beloved Psalm 23, popularly called "The Lord Is My Shepherd." The shepherd doesn't provide a giant insurance policy; rather, he is our Savior who is with us in the valley of the shadow of death that he himself endured, and who will lead us ultimately into the green pastures of eternal happiness. As a matter of fact, even an insurance policy doesn't guarantee that your house won't burn down but only that you will be compensated later.

A careful reader will not be satisfied yet. What about all that suffering that comes not from free-will decisions of angels and humans but from nature? Couldn't God have made nature without any painful aspects to it?

Lewis came up with an intriguing insight here also. He claims that to have free-will creatures with bodies (such as humans), there has to be some kind of natural background. A body needs food, shelter, clothing. Now, a piece of rock honed sharp enough to cut can also pierce the skin of someone you want to murder. The natural being, the rock, is not at fault; it is our free will that uses it wrongly. The rains that are necessary for crops to grow can become floods. Earthquakes needed to restore balance to huge underground plates can also destroy houses. This is an ecologically framed answer. Some present-day economists point out that many old tribal customs are the result of individual tribes preparing for all eventualities (such as drought and flooding) by storing necessities. The terrible sufferings of nations nowadays come largely, according to these students of society, from inequitable and inefficient ways of distributing wealth brought on by modernization. For instance, peoples who stop growing beans and rice in order to specialize in strawberries and asparagus for exportation to richer countries usually find themselves lacking in necessities in times of drought. We have the technology to rush emergency aid to any nation on earth, but we often lack the will to organize distribution effectively.

Theologians add that with the fall of mankind into original sin, nature fell as well, as understood in the famous passage of St. Paul where he tells of all "creation . . . groaning . . . [for] the coming of the redemption of our bodies" (Romans 8:22-23). All creation includes the animal kingdom, which fell because of mankind.

And yet, and yet, and yet . . . that much pain? Do we need that much pain? Lewis himself had to ask that question when his beloved wife died of cancer. Suddenly all his arguments in *The Problem of Pain* seemed meaningless to him. His grief was so great that he began to imagine that, after all, God might be some demon torturing us. Like Job of the Old Testament he wished that he himself were dead: "Why give life to those bitter of heart, who long for a death that never comes. . . ?" Ultimately Job was saved from despair not by reasoning but by the overwhelming experience of the presence of God. So, too, did Lewis slowly gain strength not from his own reasoning but from God's grace.

Let us bring in here another witness — perhaps unexpected for those who know Oscar Wilde only as a witty playwright and not for the lines he penned when cast into prison on charges of homosexual seduction of the young. Once incarcerated, this lively, brilliant lover of life found Christ waiting for him behind bars. Reading the New Testament he converted to the Catholic religion, sinned again once released, yet sought the Church's sacraments on his deathbed. Here is what he wrote in the famous *De Profundis:*

> I used to say that there was enough suffering in one narrow London lane to show that God did not love man, and that wherever there was any sorrow, though but that of a child, in some little garden weeping over a fault that it had or had not committed, the whole face of creation was completely marred. I was entirely wrong. I was not in the sphere in which belief was to be attained to.
>
> Now it seems to me that love of some kind is the only explanation of the extraordinary amount of suffering that there is in the world. I cannot conceive of any other explanation. I am convinced that there is no other, and that if the world has indeed, as I have said, been built of sorrow, it has been built by the hands of love, because in no other way could the soul of man, for whom the world was made, reach the full stature of its perfection. Pleasure for the beautiful body, but pain for the beautiful soul.

In the concentration camps of the Nazis some Jews such as Viktor Frankl were able to find meaning in suffering, a meaning that eventually brought him years afterward to belief in Christ. The Protestant woman Corrie Ten Boom, who was tortured in the camp for having hidden Jews in her house in Holland, told those in despair of God's love: "If you know Jesus, you don't have to know why."

Ultimately, Catholics believe, it is the sufferings of Jesus on the Cross that stand as a mute answer to all those who would deny God because their pain has been so great. The voluntary suffering of the God-made-man proves that God does not watch our pain from a distance, wondering if we will keep a stiff upper lip through it all. No! God himself came to earth to show that in his love he shares our suffering and wants to bring us to the only place where there will be no more pain, only joy. What does the ticket to that "magic kingdom" cost? Only that our horror of suffering may help us to try to alleviate it, following the guidance of Jesus, the Savior.

TELL ME WHY I SHOULD BE A CATHOLIC WHEN...

I'm not even sure that Jesus was divine?

The most important question a human being can ask is this: "Was Jesus divine?" The answer to that question changes the course of a person's life as surely as time and history are divided into "BC" (before Christ) and "AD" (*anno Domini*, Latin for "in the year of the Lord" — that is, after Christ was born).

One day Jesus asked his disciples, "Who do people say that the Son of Man is?" They answered, "Some say John the Baptist, but others Elijah, and still others Jeremiah or one of the prophets." Then Jesus said to them, "But who do you say that I am?" The disciples probably were not yet sure about how to answer the question. Perhaps they had not been with Jesus long enough. But suddenly Peter answered, "You are the Messiah, the Son of the living God." Jesus then said to Peter, "Blessed are you, Simon son of Jonah! For flesh and blood has not revealed this to you, but my Father in heaven. And I tell you, you are Peter [which means rock], and on this rock I will build my church and . . . I will give you the keys of the kingdom of heaven, . . ." (Refer to Matthew 16:13-19.)

In that incident, Jesus realizes that God has given Peter the *personal revelation* to know who Jesus is and that he is divine. Elsewhere in the Scriptures we see many cases of people coming to believe in the divinity of Jesus by the *grace of faith*. And we see still others *reasoning* their way to accepting that he is divine. Our own lives are reflections of the Scriptures. Some of us have had the remarkable grace of a personal revelation from God as to the divinity of Jesus; millions of us have been given the gift-grace of faith in him; yet others have reasoned the case for and against the divinity of Jesus. Those, then, are the three ways that people come to faith in Christ as divine: personal revelation, grace of faith, and reasoning.

While we will concentrate here on the *reasons* offered to show that Jesus was indeed divine, we know that accepting Jesus as the Lord and Savior is a matter of grace, the gift of loving trust in him. Dr. Alexis Carrel, a Frenchman working in the area of medical research in New York during the Second World War, won the Nobel Prize in physiology and medicine. A rigorous scientist, he mapped out the psychiatric and genetic plan[1] the world needs in order that humans may be rulers of their universe. His ideas were much acclaimed and still are. Later in life he became a member of the International Medical Bureau at Lourdes. There, being involved in evaluating as an agnostic scientist a medically unexplainable cure, his reason forced him to face the fact of the supernatural at work. And what was the supernatural at work? It was prayer — prayer answered by Mary, the Mother of Jesus, through the power of her Son. That is how an agnostic Nobel Prize winner was led by reason to the divinity of Jesus. Then, in response to his own fervent prayers, faith followed.

Peter, the one who had answered Jesus correctly, was only a poor fisherman. When we meet him again after the return of Jesus to heaven he is so filled with the power of the divine Jesus that all conditions of people flock to his teaching and to his miraculous curative powers. But, in reality, it is the power of the divine Jesus at work in Peter.

"Peter looked intently at him [a physically disabled man who wanted money], as did John and said, 'Look at us.' And he fixed his attention on them, expecting to receive something from them. But Peter said, 'I have no silver or gold, but what I have I give you; in the name of Jesus Christ of Nazareth, stand up and walk!' And he took him by the right hand and raised him up; and immediately his feet and ankles were made strong. Jumping up, he stood and began to walk. . ." (Acts 3:4-8).

So great is the divine power present in Peter and the apostles that people flock to them for all kinds of cures. In consequence, "more and more believers, men and women in great numbers" (see Acts 5:14) come to faith in Jesus. Even Peter's shadow, falling on the sick as he passed by, could cure in the name of Jesus. Whether we are talking of Lourdes today or the Holy Land of Peter's day, the divinity of Jesus is proven in the miracles and wonders wrought in his name.

Jesus himself, of course, worked miracles personally: all kinds of miracles, from the small to the great. Humans may perform miracles in the name of God or Jesus; Jesus performs the small and the stupendous in his own name. One day, "A leper came to him [Jesus] begging him, and kneeling he said to him, 'If you choose, you can make me clean.'

Moved with pity, Jesus . . . said, 'I do choose. Be made clean' " (Mark 1:40-41). He cures the blind, the lame, the dumb, the paralytic. He even raises his friend Lazarus from the grave and gives him back to his sisters (see John 11:1-43).

In the Lazarus event, Jesus tells Lazarus's sister Martha: "I am the resurrection and the life" (John 11:25). He means that he not only has the power of life and death, he is actually the power of life itself. Before that, "Jesus said to her, 'Your brother will rise again.' Martha said to him, 'I know that he will rise again in the resurrection on the last day' " (John 11:23-24).

No other human in history has shown the power of raising the truly dead to life — only Jesus. And his power is even more startling. On several occasions before different audiences he states that he will raise himself from his own biological death and that he will live eternally. He has then not only resurrection power over our ordinary lives but over his very own. No such man — whether he be prophet, founder of a religion, king, or scientist — has ever even dared to suggest such power.

Did Jesus do it? The record is given in the twenty-fourth chapter of Luke's gospel. It describes the first meetings of humans with the risen Jesus. They all have difficulty recognizing him at first because it is the same Jesus they knew before, but in some way he is changed. Gradually, we see that the "change" is that of a body that is now touched with glory.

Jesus' miracles were performed to help people in response to their physical and spiritual needs. He had immense compassion for people, and he responded to those who asked him — *with faith* —

45

for their cure. This is a necessity. You must ask in great trust and faith. And you must *ask*. "Ask and it will be given to you; seek and you will find; knock and the door will be opened to you" Jesus teaches us (Matthew 7:7, *New American Bible*).

Even though Jesus' miracles were performed on behalf of needy people and in response to their trust in him, St. John notes that the miracles have an added function. They are "signs." This is the term John uses often to describe the miracles of Jesus. They are *signs of his divinity*, signs that he is the promised Messiah, signs that the Father attests to everything Jesus says and does, and signs of the divine power of Jesus over suffering, nature, and life and death.

Two things can be said of the teaching of Jesus: (1) it is magnificent, and (2) it is of God. What Jesus said spellbound people, "for he taught them as one having authority [the authority of God], and not as their scribes" (Matthew 7:29). And his teaching was attested to by numerous signs and miracles.

Did Jesus actually ever *say* that he was divine? Not in that language; but, yes, in other language. As we saw, he calls Peter blessed for acknowledging that he is the Son of God. The gospels show us a Jesus who claims to be greater than the temple (that is, the house of the presence of God) (Matthew 12:6); to be greater than the Sabbath, to be even Lord over the Sabbath (Matthew 12:8); to be greater than the holy law that governs God's people (Matthew 5:27-28). Jesus claims to be above the angels (Matthew 13:41) and — most important — equal to God the Father (Matthew 11:27). He claimed to be the Messiah (John 4:25-26). In claiming to be the one who will judge the living and the dead, the judge of Bible prophecy, he is claiming to be God (Matthew 25:31-46).

He interprets and enlarges the law given Moses by God (Matthew 5:20ff). He states flatly, "All authority in heaven and on earth has been given to me" (Matthew 28:18). He points out that he and the Father are one, that those who see him see the Father (refer to John 14:8-12). And in John 5:36 the Lord says that the works he performs testify that he is from God in the same equality of being.

The message Jesus has for us and for the world is the message from God for us. That becomes the ultimate meaning of "the signs and wonders" Jesus wrought to authenticate his mission and to turn us to the Father through Jesus.

Jesus forgave sin. Only God can forgive sin. This may not impress us moderns, but it should. Because the Jewish people were perfectly aware that only God is God; that only God can forgive sin; and that the ultimate blasphemy is for a human (no matter how holy or how brilliant) to claim the power of forgiving sin. But Jesus claimed it — and used a miracle to prove his claim. The dramatic incident, as recorded in Mark 2:3-12, follows:

[While Jesus was delivering God's word to them], some people came, bringing to him a paralyzed man, carried by four of them. And when they could not bring him to Jesus because of the crowd, they removed the roof above him; and after having dug through it, they let down the mat on which the paralytic lay. When Jesus saw their faith, he said to the paralytic, "Son, your sins are forgiven." Now some of the scribes were sitting there, questioning in their hearts, "Why does this fellow speak in this way? It is blasphemy! Who can forgive sins but God alone?" At once Jesus perceived in his spirit that they were discussing these questions among themselves; and he said to them, "Why do you raise such questions in your hearts? Which is easier, to say to the paralytic, 'Your sins are forgiven,' or to say, 'Stand up and take your mat and walk'? But so that you may know that the Son of Man has authority on earth to forgive sins" — he said to the paralytic — "I say to you, stand up, take your mat and go to your home." And he stood up, and immediately took the mat and went out before all of them; so that they were amazed and glorified God, saying, "We have never seen anything like this!"

This would have been the ultimate blasphemy, indeed, if Jesus had been just a holy man. But he was not just a holy Person, he was a divine Person.

Jesus as Messiah is the fulfillment of the promise of a Savior. His actual life, in its personal pain, is the awful burden of fulfilling the prophesies of the Servant of God and the Suffering Servant.[2] As such, Jesus must endure passion and death to save us. His sufferings flesh out the portrait of the Redeemer, the God-man, drawn centuries earlier by Jeremiah and Isaiah. It is the God-man who is born at Bethlehem. "Look, the virgin shall conceive and bear a son, and they shall call him Emmanuel, which means 'God is with us' " (Matthew 1:23). It is the same Jesus who is exalted as God by the early Christians when they call him by God's name — "Lord." As St. Paul exhorts us: ". . . at the name of

Jesus every knee should bend, in heaven and on earth and under the earth, and every tongue should confess that Jesus Christ is Lord, to the glory of God the Father" (Philippians 2:10-11).

In his classic work, *Grammar of Assent*,[3] Cardinal Newman clothes the reflections of the great Napoleon in these words as the emperor sits in the solitude of his prison:

> I have been accustomed to put before me the examples of Alexander and Caesar, with a hope of rivalling their exploits, and living in the minds of men forever. Yet, after all, in what sense does Caesar, in what sense does Alexander live? At best, nothing but their names is known. . . . No, even their names do but flit up and down the world like ghosts, mentioned only on particular occasions, or from accidental associations. Their chief home is the schoolroom; they have a foremost place in boys' grammars and exercise books. . . . So low is heroic Alexander fallen, so low is imperial Caesar. . . .
>
> But, on the contrary, there is just one Name in the whole world that lives; it is the name of One Who passed His years in obscurity, and Who died a malefactor's death. Eighteen hundred years have gone since that time, but still it has its hold on the human mind. It has possessed the world, and it maintains possession. Amid the most varied nations, under the most diversified circumstances, in the most cultivated, in the rudest races and intellects, in all classes of society, the Owner of that great Name reigns. High and low, rich and poor, acknowledge Him. Millions of souls are conversing with Him, are venturing on His word, are looking for His presence.

Palaces [church buildings] sumptuous, innumerable, are raised to His honour; His image, as
in the hour of His deepest humiliation, is triumphantly displayed in the proud city, in the open
country, in the corners of streets, on the tops of
mountains. It sanctifies the ancestral hall, and the
bedchamber; it is the subject for the exercise of the
highest genius in the imitative arts. It is worn next
to the heart in life; it is held before the failing eyes in
death. Here, then, is One Who is *not* a mere name,
Who is not a mere fiction, Who is a reality.

He is dead and gone, but still He lives, — lives as
a living, energetic thought of successive generations,
as the awful motive power of a thousand great
events. He has done without effort what others with
life-long struggles have not done. Can He be less
than divine? Who is He but the Creator Himself,
Who is sovereign over His own works, towards
Whom our eyes and hearts turn instinctively, because He is our Father and our God?

As Archbishop M. Cronin wrote of that passage,
"The argument may be put briefly as follows: The
power of Christ over the hearts of men is no natural
phenomenon. It is miraculous. It is God's testimony
to the divinity of Christ."[4]

A remarkable example of a person who came to
believe in the divinity of Christ is Blessed Francis
Libermann. He was born Jacob Libermann in the
early nineteenth century in Alsace, France, into a
rabbinical family. Jacob was the fifth son of a father
totally devoted to the teaching of the Jewish religion,
a father who hoped that *all* of his sons would follow
in his footsteps as rabbis.

At that time, young Jewish boys were constantly warned about the persecution they might experience at the hands of the Christians of their cities and towns. They were told that even looking at the figure of "that naked man on the cross" might open them up to the influence of demons, and that terrible consequences might follow wandering into a church even out of curiosity.

It was also a time when many Jewish young people were breaking away from the ways of the ghetto and seeking to become part of European culture, sometimes by assimilating Gentile ways and even becoming baptized as Catholics and Protestants.

Jacob's father did everything in his power to prevent such an outcome for his children. However, it was considered a necessity for the education of a good rabbi that he spend some time away from his village in a big city where he could sit at the feet of the great Jewish scholars of the day, then bring that wisdom back home with him.

One by one old Rabbi Lazarus Libermann sent his sons to the city to be perfected in Jewish wisdom. The first son decided to study medicine instead. His father cut him off. Mingling in medical circles, this son soon met non-Jews and discovered that many of them were not as evil as those who started pogroms and other persecutions. Indeed, some were good and very spiritual. Eventually, after great struggle, he and his wife became Catholics. His old father went into mourning. Two other sons went to the city and they also became Catholics.

In an agony of horror, the rabbi concentrated all his attention on the most brilliant of his sons, Jacob. But when Jacob went off to Metz to study, all of a sudden what he was learning became stale and then doubtful. It happened that at this time Jacob was teaching Hebrew to a friend. To his surprise, the friend chose the New Testament in Hebrew as the reader. Jacob read it cover to cover. At first he was not much impressed: the figure of Jesus seemed beautiful to him, but the miracles seemed like fairy tales.

Yet certain passages — especially the beatitudes — began to work their way into the young man's soul. When he visited his elder brother, the doctor, he was amazed at the new softness in his character since his baptism. Bewildered, Jacob began to become frightened about his own future. Rabbinic Judaism no longer appealed to him. Christianity seemed wonderful but unbelievable.

He went to consult a certain Rabbi Drach who had converted in Paris and was teaching Hebrew at a Roman Catholic seminary. Drach suggested that he stay at the seminary for a while and study with him. In the middle of the night, Jacob could stand it no longer. Tortured by doubt, he prayed with tears: "O Eternal God of my fathers, enlighten me and lift the misery in which I wander, forlorn and alone. If this Christ is in truth Your Son and the Messiah, make it so known to me. But if this teaching is false, I beseech Thee, God of my fathers, save me from the abyss over which I tremble."[5]

Presently, his doubt was lifted and his heart liberated as if "by a mighty force."[6] He believed.

Later on, Jacob Libermann became Father Francis Libermann. He founded a new order of missionaries in the Church and was beatified for his holiness.

C. S. Lewis was another man who discovered the divinity of Christ after much doubt. This famous English professor of the classics of our century had been raised a Protestant but had fallen into skepticism during his youth. Throughout this time he tended to think that Jesus was a good man, indeed the best of men, a great sage, but surely not God incarnate. Meeting up with certain Christians at Oxford who seemed to be both virtuous and intelligent, he began to question his own philosophy about Jesus.

In *Mere Christianity* Lewis sums up the fruit of his reflections. Jesus claimed that he was God incarnate. This was especially striking because he wasn't born into a tradition where all spiritual people thought of themselves as having a spark of the divine in them. Indeed, Jesus' claim was considered to be blasphemy. But do we think that a man who claims to be God is a great sage, or would we ourselves tend to think that he was a liar or an insane man? Think about it. A friend you deeply admire takes you aside one day and tells you his great secret, "I am God." Would you be delighted to hear it or would you be deeply shocked and doubtful about him? You wouldn't think it one further proof of how good he was.

So, Lewis tells us — make a choice: either Jesus is who he says he is, God; or he is not a good man at all but either a liar or insane. Since nothing about his character would give the impression that he was a liar or insane, we must seriously confront ourselves with the probability that he was actually God-made-man. We cannot sit on the fence by claiming that he was a wonderful prophet and sage.

Lewis put his faith in Jesus being who he said he was.

ENDNOTES

1. Alexis Carrel, *Man, The Unknown* (New York: Harper Brothers, 1939).
2. Servant passages in regard to the Redeemer to come are found in the book of the prophet Isaiah (esp. chs. 42-44).
3. J. H. Newman, *Grammar of Assent* (London: Longman's, 1878).
4. The passage from Newman and the concluding comment are given in Most Rev. M. Sheehan, *Apologetics & Catholic Doctrine* (Dublin: M. H. Gill & Son, 1952), pp. 118-119.
5. Helen Walker Homan, *Star of Jacob* (New York: David McKay Co., 1953), p. 161.
6. Ibid.

TELL ME WHY I SHOULD BE A CATHOLIC WHEN...

the Church has such a history of evil to her name?

To some observers there is no organization in the world with a worse record than the Catholic Church! The very words "Roman Catholic," far from conveying images of great saints, remind such critics of tales of persecutions, inquisitions, religious wars, scandalous popes of the past, and despicable priests of the present.

How could a church devoted to following the teachings of the Prince of Peace be so violent? How could followers of a Savior who was so pure give in so frequently to sexual sin? How could disciples of a Master who lived so poorly luxuriate in palaces?

The earliest history of believers in Jesus was marked not by sins of violence perpetrated by Christians but by martyrdom of Christ's followers at the hands of others. It was only when Christians became politically powerful that they were in a position to resolve disputes by force of arms.

Some wars were defensive and were waged against barbarian invasions; others involved battles over religious ideas. When there was a conflict between groups professing differing ideas about the nature of the Trinity or about Christ, and each group included powerful political figures, the situation was ripe for attempts to enforce unanimity through violence!

Eventually many thought that if Church leaders themselves were chosen from the upper governing classes, greater harmony between Church and state would prevail. It was not long before one could find bishops and popes of little or no piety, chosen for political reasons.

It has always been a temptation for religious leaders of all faiths to seek the help of the state in the promotion of religious institutions. The results seem always to be ruinous, for power always tends to corrupt. Here is an example from our times: many religious colleges want federal aid for their students. But to retain this aid, they often believe they must secularize their schools by omitting prayer from classes not directly about theology, or by tolerating dissenting forms of pluralism to avoid any possible charges concerning lack of academic freedom. You might note that contemporary examples of worldly reasoning often seem less shocking than those of the past, because our own compromises fit our cultural mind-set and therefore seem readily forgivable!

At the worst times of the past, elections of popes took months and even years as outside forces tried to poison the food of candidates deemed unlikely to further the selfish projects of princes and emperors. Other abuses included nepotism (handing out Church offices to nephews and other relatives in order to benefit the extended family in financial ways and also ensure allies) and simony (selling of holy things such as indulgences). Although such practices seem foreign and almost bizarre to moderns, a close reading of Church history makes it easy to see how they developed from innocent to evil. To translate into contemporary life, let us suppose you were president of the United States. What would be more natural than to put into your cabinet a young nephew who was politically ambitious as well as good? This could easily lead to other members of your extended family expecting similar opportunities even if they were not especially suited for the posts in question. Or, suppose you are a priest eager to renovate your parish church. Your flock is eager to participate through contributions, but you still need a little more to purchase the marvelous organ you saw on sale a month ago. Would it seem *so* evil to tell the congregation that you will say special prayers for the dead in those families who contributed more than one hundred dollars to the fund? It might seem like a bright idea until you realize that it could lead later to greater and greater abuses such as in the case of the lavish works of art found in great cathedrals now admired even by those Protestants (originally, protesting Catholics) who were so rightfully horrified by the sale of indulgences for the building of cathedrals at the time of the Reformation!

Happily in our times popes have little worldly power and the last century and a half have seen one holy pope after another.

The story of the Crusades is also a sad one. There is documentation to prove that Church leaders planned these excursions for holy reasons. They believed that if the warlike knights could be sent to rescue the Holy Land from Muslims they would cease their local feuding. The knights of the Crusades were taught to avoid all unnecessary bloodshed and certainly to avoid the sins of looting and rape so prevalent in medieval times as well as in modern times. Unfortunately, most of the crusaders fell into the temptation of indulging in atrocities in spite of all warnings to the contrary. Wars, whether religiously motivated or not, always include atrocities. After all, atheistic states such as the Soviet Union were responsible for far greater atrocities toward enemies — and citizens.

Indeed, a close reading of the Holy Scripture reveals how the chosen people repeatedly rejected the covenant and sank into immoral practices. Cycles of fervor followed by commitment to God and then by betrayal, punishment, repentance, and reform are also characteristic, alas, of the history of all churches.

Of all the sins of people belonging to the Catholic Church the ones most distressing to potential con-verts concern the relationship of Catholics and Jews. In the early days of the Church, Christian Jews were afraid of Jews who had not accepted Jesus as the Messiah.

Later on, more and more Gentiles became Chris-tians. As the Church became more powerful in the Roman Empire during the reign of Constantine, Catholics would often see the Jews among them as potential enemies — people not united by belief in Christ who might form an alliance with the enemies of Catholic emperors and kings. Living often in separate areas of cities, partly because they them-selves wanted to be with kinsmen, Jews would sometimes become objects of envy if they were rich and subjected to violence by those wanting to steal their goods.

Most terrible was the way greedy Catholics and

other Christians would time their looting and killing to coincide with religious holidays that could be used as a pretext for their riotous attacks on Jews. Based on the passages in Scripture about Caiaphas handing Jesus over to the Romans for crucifixion, irrational Catholic and Orthodox rabble would rush out of church on Good Friday to persecute and even kill innocent Jewish people. Such pogroms continued well into the twentieth century and have left an enduring mark of fear even in the hearts of Jews who have never known persecution personally.

Other forms of persecution and intimidation of Jews by Catholics had to do with political motives linked to religious issues. For example, in Spain where many Jews lived for centuries in prosperity and peace, the situation changed dramatically during the centuries of Muslim incursions into southern Spain. In those times it was feared that Arabs would take over all of Europe.

Mounting a holy war, or crusade, against the Muslims, the Spanish royalty such as Ferdinand and Isabella needed to be sure of the loyalty of all peoples in their kingdom. Could they count on the Jews? They were not sure. They worried particularly about the Marranos — Jews who converted to the Catholic faith, some because of a religious conversion to Christ but others purely as a defensive political move to consolidate their position in society. These practiced Judaism secretly in their homes.

It was not irrational to think that such phony converts might join forces with Muslims in a crisis if they thought it in their best interests. Since Isabella and Ferdinand actually favored Jewish converts as members of their court, it became critical to find out which converts were loyal and which shaky.

A way to decide appeared in the form of the inquisition. Set up to deal with Christian heretics, it was originally designed to protect the *innocent* by means of theological questioning by trusted Dominican theologians who were to substitute rational means for the type of torture so prevalent in all states at that time. The Church was not to be involved in punishment but only in making a judgment as to whether a person was heretical or not. Since heresy was deemed not only a danger to the Church but primarily to order in the state (that is, treason), in that heretics set up rival groups in collusion with foreign princes, it would be up to the state to punish the heretic.

Our most vivid image of the link between political factors and religious judicial procedures can be found in the trial and death of Joan of Arc. Even such unbiased chroniclers as George Bernard Shaw and Mark Twain, certainly not predisposed toward the Catholic Church, show in their portrayals how the real issue was not Catholic doctrine but political factors pitting the French allies of the invading English against loyalist French.

Going back to the Spanish inquisition, it was fear of internal traitors that led Isabella and Ferdinand to employ Dominican priests to determine which Jewish converts were sincere, with subsequent torture, death, or banishment of the insincere. There is evidence that figures about the number of Jews burned at the stake are highly exaggerated, having been written up by a disaffected ex-Catholic and then quoted ever since to blacken the record of

Church practices. But even so, the picture remains terrible and terrifying.

Religious wars between Protestants and Catholics were common in the sixteenth and seventeenth centuries. Many of these wars were political more than religious. A prince who wanted to get out from under the temporal power of the pope had only to become a Protestant to acquire all the property of the Catholic Church in his lands. If there was resistance, this would lead to warfare.

To people of the United States deeply imbued with ideals of religious tolerance, such wars seem incredible. Even though we also have quite a history of persecution, particularly of Native Americans and Afro-Americans as well as Catholics, never have we seen anything resembling the Thirty Years' War in Europe from 1618 to 1648. Some of us view with disgust the battles going on between Protestants and Catholics in Northern Ireland, imagining they are fighting only because of distaste for each other's religion. Such is not the case. Economics and politics are the key to the violence. Religion merely parallels the long-standing inequalities in that country. It should be noted that the IRA (Irish Republican Army) has many times been condemned and its members excommunicated by the Catholic Church for its vengeful violence. Similar action has not been taken against the gunmen on the other side.

Of course, whenever a nation is convinced that its wars are just, its citizens do not think of themselves as violent. In our century we in the United States have been in almost constant war: World War I, World War II, Korea, Vietnam, Panama, the Gulf War.

In our own century the Nazi Holocaust, attempting to rid the whole world of its Jews, has been seen by many as a travesty rooted in previous religiously motivated anti-Semitism. No matter how much documentation we have from Jewish sources of heroic self-sacrifice in the efforts of some Protestants and Catholics to save Jews, it still remains true that many Christians preferred to save themselves than to reach out to those in terrible danger. This should not surprise Catholics of our time, for how many are willing even to peacefully picket an abortion clinic at no risk whatsoever? If this is true, how harshly should those be judged who to help Jewish neighbors during World War II would have ended up going to a concentration camp to their deaths?

It is important to read some of the documentation available about those whom the Jewish survivors of World War II call "the righteous of the nations," that is, those non-Jews who *did* risk their lives to help. Many members of the Catholic Church hierarchy roused the people to resist Nazism. The man who was to become Pope John XXIII forged thousands of baptismal certificates to enable Jews to escape to Israel via Bulgaria were he was papal nuncio. A booklet entitled *Pius XII's Defence of Jews and Others: 1944-45* by Robert R. Graham, S.J. (published by the Catholic League for Religious and Civil Rights, Milwaukee; longer version — *Pius XII and the Holocaust: A Reader* by Robert A. Graham and Joseph L. Lichten, also by the same publisher), addresses itself specifically to refuting the charges made by some against Pope Pius XII that he was negligent in defending the Jews, whereas in fact he worked tirelessly underground to save as many as possible.

Here is one of many telling quotations from page 2 of this booklet: "In 1937, when leaders of the Western democracies were scurrying to Munich to negotiate with Hitler, the Holy See condemned the theory and practice of the 'Nationalist State' in the encyclical *Mit brennender Sorge* [To the bishops of Germany: On the Church and the German Reich]. When Jews felt the cruel sting of Nazi hatred, the German bishops protested, 'Whoever wears a human face owns rights which no power on earth is permitted to take away,' echoing Pius XI's declaration, 'We are all spiritual Semites.' . . . While Britain and the United States were refusing to admit refugees to their territories, the Holy See was distributing thousands of false documents — life-saving passports to freedom — to the beleaguered Jews. . . . Catholic priests, nuns and lay people were hiding Jews in their flight to safety, and often paying for it with their lives. . . . It could be asked whether these good works (praised by many European rabbis) were enough, whether it would have been better for the Pope to have denounced from the rooftops the crimes that were occurring. This thought troubled Pius XII, and he confided afterward to an associate, 'No doubt a protest would have gained me the praise and respect of many,' but he believed that such protest would only have led to more deaths whereas underground work would save lives." (Refer also to Henri de Lubac's *Christian Resistance to Anti-Semitism: Memories from 1940-1944*; New York: The Miriam Press, 1990.)

Does all of this miserable history add up to a

proof that the Catholic religion leads people into bigotry, persecution, torture, and murder? Of course not. What it comes down to is realizing that sin is always possible. When we, as members of the Church, commit sin by going against the Church's teachings, this does not mean that the whole Church is evil. It simply means that individual members are failing in their efforts to follow the Lord as they should, and people suffer as a result.

Some words of Pope John Paul II about the Holocaust display the Catholic sense of the Cross in its universal application:

> The history of Europe is marked by discord not only in the sphere of states and politics. In conjunction with political interests and social problems, these have resulted in bitter fighting, in the oppression and expulsion of dissenters, in repression and intolerance. As heirs to our forebears, we also place this guilt-ridden Europe under the Cross. For in the Cross is our hope. . . .
>
> Let us pray together (Catholics and Jews) that it (the Holocaust) will never happen again . . . it makes us still more aware of the abyss which humanity can fall into when we do not acknowledge other people as brothers and sisters, sons and daughters, of the same heavenly father.
>
> It is the teaching of both the Hebrew and Christian Scriptures that the Jews are beloved of God, who has called them with an irrevocable calling. No valid theological justification could ever be found for acts of discrimination or persecution against Jews. In fact, such acts must be held to be sinful.
>
> [This is taken from John Paul II's *On the Holo-*

caust, edited by Eugene J. Fisher, Secretariat for Catholic-Jewish Relations, National Conference of Catholic Bishops, Washington, D.C., 1988.]

With all the explanations we can come up with as to why someone might think something that is absolutely wrong is justified, there still remains the fact that violence is always an appealing solution to those under pressure of their own uncontrolled emotions of fear or greed. No religious group has a monopoly on evil or on good in terms of behavior of their people under stress.

Does this mean that, since in every religion we can find a history of atrocities, we should not be part of any religious group? First of all, such a solution to the problem conceals the premise that I, by myself, am perfect and would not act wrongly under stress of any kind! In reality, most people are much better in terms of ethical actions when they are surrounded by groups who profess principles of goodness and also provide supernatural motives for living up to these principles.

An analogy may help. Most North Americans of the United States feel proud to call themselves Americans in spite of our terrible history of negation of basic rights of Native Americans and Afro-Americans. Why? Why not flee to another country with a better historical record? If pressed, most Americans would say that it is because we believe that our Constitution is good despite the fact that some Americans have violated its spirit in the past.

In a similar way, we can love a church that teaches love even if some of its members do what is unloving. The Catholic Church, in fact, does not claim that all her members are good and holy. Quite the opposite! We are told about our need for cleansing and purification. Even popes, bishops, priests, and nuns are expected to seek sacramental reconciliation for their sins.

Within the Church we have the remedy for evil: the word of God and the sacraments. The millions of good Catholics throughout all times who have done God's will out of love for family and neighbor were living up to their faith. The ones who succumbed to evil were betraying it.

Looking back to the accounts in the gospels, would you have joined the band around Jesus yourself, or would you have stayed far away to avoid the company of Judas? If you would have joined the followers of Jesus then, be part of his Church now!

Similar reasoning may help in confronting the problem of the sexual sins of Catholics, especially those sins that hit the history books and newspapers for their scandalousness. We naturally wish that everyone who makes a good promise would keep it, especially when the breaking of it involves the victimization of others. Whenever Catholics — single or married — sin in a sexual manner, it is scandalous and injurious not only to the victims but also to themselves. But when a priest, Sister, or Brother does so, it seems to strike Catholics and non-Catholics even more forcefully. To even imagine promising chastity is something so noble that failure to live up to it may seem even worse. Also there enters into the picture the problem of the victim often being a young person whose trust has been violated.

Sad, distressing, and agonizing as such sins are,

are they reason to leave the Catholic Church or to stay away from her? Again, the failure to live up to an ideal is not a reason to throw out the ideal. When a Catholic prays the Apostles' Creed, he or she does not say, "I believe in Father X or Sister Y or Brother Z." Nor does someone enter into love relationships or marriage because he or she has only seen holy models of chastity and fidelity. Praying for God's grace, we should try to avoid all sin ourselves and we should also pray for and support anyone, whether the individual is a leader or not, who seems to be struggling with temptation or to have given in to it. How much sexual sin results from loneliness — loneliness that could have been somewhat alleviated by our friendship!

Next, under the topic of evils of the Church, comes the question of luxury of Church art or of the clergy's lifestyle in the face of the needs of the poor. Over and over again in the history of the Church, reformers have asked: "Why not sell all the gold in Church art, sell grand buildings, and give the money to the poor?" Jesus was poor, so why are his priests decked out in jeweled crowns, their standard of living sometimes higher than the people they minister to?

Jesus himself seems to have given a partial answer in Mark 14:3ff when some asked why a costly perfume was being poured out on his head when the perfume could have been sold and the money given to the poor. Jesus replied that the poor are always with us, but that this was something special, since the woman pouring the perfume was anointing his body in preparation for its burial.

Traveling around the world and visiting beautiful

cathedrals, one is not given the impression that the people of the towns and cities think of the cathedral as something belonging to the priest or bishop or the pope. Rather, they regard the church as theirs. Poor as they may be, they can, if they wish, visit daily their "spiritual living room," reflecting the glory of the life to come in heaven.

This attitude might be compared to the way a poor married woman might cling to the gold ring on her finger as the last thing she would sell even to provide necessities. The ring symbolizes for her how important the bond of love is, even more important than the "daily bread," which would in any case disappear within a a relatively short time after the sale of her treasure.

Great Church architecture, art, music, vestments, chalices, lace altar clothes — all these indicate that important as social justice is, beauty is also a hunger of the human soul. "One does not live by bread alone" (Matthew 4:4).

* * *

Among those who became Catholics knowing full well the evils of particular Catholics in history, some of the most striking conversions are of Jewish people. Realizing that Jesus, Mary, Joseph, and the apostles as well as most of the early disciples were Jewish, they are thrilled to complete their Jewish heritage by accepting their Messiah and his Church.

Of more recent European Hebrew-Catholics we have Blessed Edith Stein, Blessed Francis Libermann, Raïssa Maritain, Venerable Hermann Cohen, Max Picard, John Osterreicher, Father Alphonse

Ratisbonne, and Rabbi Israel Zolli. From the United States, among the most well-known are Karl Stern, Father Raphael Simon, Charles Rich, and Father Arthur Klyber. Father Elias Friedman is a South African who is now a Carmelite monk at Mount Carmel near Haifa in Israel. He is the founder of the International Hebrew Catholic Association.

For information about these and other Jewish converts to the Catholic faith see *The Ingrafting* (New Hope, Ky.: Remnant of Israel, 1987), which I edited, and four booklets (*He's a Jew; This Jew; Queen of the Jews; Once a Jew*), edited by Father Arthur Klyber, also published by Remnant of Israel.

Of those converts with a burning desire to help the poor who chose to work within the Church rather than to scorn her as unworthy, the one who stands out the most in our century might be Dorothy Day, founder of the Catholic Worker movement. At the time of her youth in the early part of the twentieth century, Dorothy had joined the Communist party hoping that social revolution could accomplish the justice that could not be found in the United States as it was. Disillusioned, she began to experience within herself a great spiritual thirst.

When she met the Catholic radical Peter Maurin, together they founded a sort of Catholic communism. They would champion the rights of workers as well as tend to the immediate needs of the poor by means of a newspaper, soup kitchens, hospitality houses, and common prayer.

Probably there is not a single Catholic saint concerned with active works to help the poor who has not felt frustration because of the apathy of some middle-class and rich Catholics toward the desperate needs of the poverty-stricken. The response of the saints, however, was not to abandon the Church but to take upon themselves the task of instituting programs for the relief of the poor by supplying food, clothing, and shelter as well as free hospitals, schools, and the like. A model of how anger at apathy can become zealous service can be found in St. Vincent de Paul of France who organized such rich ladies as St. Louise de Marillac to go out into the streets and find the orphans, the sick, the illiterate, and help them.

TELL ME WHY I SHOULD BE A CATHOLIC WHEN...

the Church is so lukewarm?

This book would be sorely incomplete if we didn't at least touch on an issue that, although simple to answer intellectually, is one of the biggest obstacles to becoming or remaining Catholic to many people: namely the seeming lack of vibrancy of the congregation at religious services as compared to the atmosphere of some Pentecostal-type churches.

If you enter the arena where Christian worship is taking place you will see thousands of ardent Christians singing loudly, clapping their hands, and listening with rapt attention to the life-changing messages of the preacher. Afterward there is likely to be an altar call with visitors rushing up to be prayed over as they give themselves heart and soul to Jesus.

A joke poking fun at Catholics revolves around a discussion between a Christian healer and a fellow minister. "I was invited by the Catholic parish to give some talks there." Fellow minister: "Why in the world would you go there to the Catholics when you have a successful healing ministry here?" Christian healer: "It's better to raise the dead than to heal the sick!"

Visiting a Catholic church, Christians of this type cannot believe that our claim that Jesus is really present in the Eucharist could be true. If he were there in some unusual way, wouldn't Catholics be at least as joyful about it as they are at a prayer meeting? Instead, why do the Catholics they see at Sunday Masses seem bored, restless, lukewarm?

Our response to these questions involves, to some extent, differing prayer styles. The quietness of most Catholic congregations has partly to do with centuries of silent reverence for the mystery of Christ entering into the bread and the wine at the Consecration being considered the deepest response of loving awe. There is also a great tradition in the Catholic Church of beautiful chant and choral music, but this was primarily sung by trained musicians or monks and nuns rather than by the congregation as a whole. After Vatican II, the liturgical movement, which championed singing by the assembly, finally bore fruit with the change from Latin to the vernacular. Many Catholics were unprepared for the change. Used to thinking that only those in the choir with "good voices" should sing, many prefer to remain quiet or to sing softly even when prompted to proclaim their faith loudly in participatory verbal response and in song.

A few decades ago, many Catholics were prayed over for the charismatic gifts of the Spirit such as tongues, prophecy, and healing. Set afire they came to pray and sing just the way Pentecostal and some Evangelical Protestants do.

Because the real presence of Christ at the Consecration and in the Holy Eucharist has always been the center of the Mass, there has not been the same emphasis on stirring preaching in the past. At this time there is much more balance in seminary training between the sacrament and the proclaiming of the word with fervor and preaching in ways that rouse the people to self-examination and conversion of action.

If anyone would care to count up the number of Catholics who come to church *every day* out of passionate love for Jesus and the Church together with those who come on Sunday out of fervor not only because it is obligatory (after all, if you can't spend one hour a week worshiping the God who gives you your whole lifetime, you can't call yourself a good Christian), this number would be equal if not greater than the number of fervent Protestants.

Why not just have the "100 percenters" in the Church then, rather than tolerate the lukewarm or sinful members? The answer is very deep and comes right from the mouth of Jesus in the parable about the self-righteous man and the sinner (see, for example, Matthew 9:9-13) as well as in Jesus' entire mission to the lost sheep (see, for instance, Matthew 18:12-14). Of course Jesus wants to set us on fire.

But he also loves those who hang in there confusedly, somehow thinking there is something good in the Church even though they are not willing right now to respond all the way to it. Many the man or woman committed to a sinful lifestyle who yet feels the least he or she can do is to worship the God of holiness. Sometimes after many years such a one accepts the grace to change his or her lifestyle, to receive once more the holy sacraments, and to come alive in praise of God's mercy. Is it the Spirit of Jesus to gather around him the best and leave everyone else out? Or is it to form a Church of mingled wheat and chaff — of saints and would-be saints, of good, bad, and indifferent, all of whom need to hear his word and be drawn to his heart?

Here is a story of someone recently received into the Catholic Church who struggled through the difficulties described in this chapter. She prefers keeping her name anonymous at this time.

I was brought up as a Catholic. I always found going to Church with my family extremely boring and religious-education classes silly. So as soon as I left home to go to college I dropped going to Church altogether, although I still used to say a Hail Mary in the morning and a night prayer for whatever was making me anxious during the day.

When I was in my late twenties one of my friends at work took me to her prayer meeting at a large auditorium. I couldn't believe how these people loved Jesus and the joy and even fun they had praying and singing. So I went up at the altar call and for five years went to their prayer meetings, Bible studies, and other teachings.

Last year, however, whenever I came to passages in the Bible about the Last Supper I started to get this craving to receive the Catholic Eucharist. When I asked my pastor, the answers he gave as to why we didn't receive regularly didn't make any sense at all.

Since the leading of the Holy Spirit got stronger and stronger, I decided to take up a long-standing invitation from another friend to go to a charismatic Mass with her.

At the words of the Consecration I was absolutely convinced that this was the truth, and that I had to return to a church where I could receive all the sacraments regularly. I have never regretted my decision because I find the sacraments so vital to my spiritual growth.

TELL ME WHY I SHOULD BE A CATHOLIC WHEN...

we live in an ecumenical age and do not see a need for everyone to belong to 'one Church'?

Just a few months ago, I received a retired Methodist pastor into the Church or, as the particular rite of reception has it, into full communion with the Catholic Church. Let us give him the name Dr. John. A pastor-educator for over thirty years, Dr. John holds among his credentials an earned doctorate in theology. His attempts to follow his conscience and grace and join the Catholic Church were met by obstacles — not from his dear family and friends but from Catholics.

First of all, there was the rectory housekeeper who didn't know enough English to field his questions as to how he should go about the process of gaining membership in the Roman Catholic faith. Then came the associate pastor who — perhaps externalizing his own inner fragmentation — said bluntly: "Why would you want to join the Catholic Church? We're more confused than you people are." Next came the pastor ("a kindly man," Dr. John said) who knew that the present catechumenate program was already under way in his parish and that Dr. John would have to wait "about two years" for the next opportunity. (This pastor didn't seem to know that a baptized Christian pastor is not a prospective catechumen, or that a much shorter rite of reception into the Church is available to already baptized Christians like Dr. John.)

A Catholic acquaintance of Dr. John directed him to the local seminary where he met a very amiable instructor who was, nonetheless, adamant that this is an ecumenical age and "in ecumenism, it is not right to seek conversion." Some time elapsed and then, one afternoon, I happened to be in my room when the secretary buzzed me — and down the stairs I went to meet the graciously persistent Dr. John.

We did not get through the first instruction session together before he asked me, "Why do so many Catholics today, especially priests, make it almost a point of honor to discourage people like me from seeking acceptance in Roman Catholicism when my conscience leads me to it?"

For reasons such as this I am not surprised that the mainline churches in America are experiencing depletion in their rosters. They are making no serious effort to win converts (may the old expression be forgiven me!). On the contrary, their erstwhile members are flocking to the voices of televangelism, Fundamentalism, and the New Age. In Catholicism, millions of Hispanic Catholics and Latino Catholics follow the charismatic Fundamentalists, yet the Catholic Church continues to report them on the lists as Catholics, without making a serious effort to win them back. But, then, in an ecumenical age does it make any difference? Are they not "saved," and are we not all equally the members of Christ's Church?

Thus far I have been describing the *de facto* pastoral misunderstanding of the meaning of ecumenism. Let us turn to the academic-theological understanding of the import of ecumenism.

Most academic theologians I read approach the Second Vatican Council's "Decree on Ecumenism" and the "Dogmatic Constitution on the Church" and see significant changes in the Catholic Church's view of herself vis-à-vis the other Christian churches. Among these changes supposedly are: that the Catholic Church no longer defines herself as the true Church; that she no longer states that membership is necessary for salvation; that the other Christian churches all compose the Catholic Church in her fullness since (it is inferred) the differences in teaching are not of a basic nature. In consequence, it is argued, the ecumenical spirit of cooperation should replace any misguided conversion ministry.

These theologians stress that neither document flatly states that the Roman Catholic Church is the true Church or the only Church of the Lord's foundation. Much is made of the "Dogmatic Constitution on the Church's" use of terms. Instead of saying that the Church of Jesus exists as the Roman Catholic Church, the document uses the phrase "subsists in" the Roman Catholic Church.[1]

No theologian should conclude from this that the Catholic Church has now reversed her dogmatic teaching on her own nature as the foundation of the Lord: one, holy, catholic, and apostolic. In an ecumenical document it is to be expected that the Roman Church should not stress her uniqueness but rather stress those similarities with all the

Christian churches that have long been seen by Rome as relating them to the Catholic Church.

Without deprecating the importance of the ecumenical movement, the following points must be considered in answering the question "Why be a Catholic in an ecumenical age?" These points are: (1) the unchangeable teaching of the Church about herself; (2) what Vatican Council II does *not* say about the Reform/Protestant churches; (3) our call to live ecclesial fullness; and (4) the right of Dr. John and others like him to seek admission into the Catholic Church.

Let us take the first point: the unchangeable teaching of the Catholic Church regarding herself. As one might guess, the Catholic Church has reflected on her own nature for the past two thousand years. She has defined many things about herself by reflecting on the Scriptures, by listening to her saints and scholars, through having to teach the faith to her children, through opposing heretical ideas, and through the authoritative definitions given in the great councils that have tied together those twenty centuries.

The Church uses two sources for speaking authoritatively about who she is and about her teachings. These are: (1) the words of God in the Scriptures, and (2) the Holy Spirit of truth given to the Church at her beginning on the first Pentecost. The God-given and continuing direction of the original Church by the Spirit ("he will guide you into all the truth" [John 16:13]) and the presence of Jesus with his bride ("I am with you always, to the end of the age" [Matthew 28:20]) are seen by the Church as divine guarantees that she cannot teach falsehood or lose her status as the only bride of Christ and the depository of the saving truth of Jesus.

Therefore, the Church sees herself as having the truth that matters and being preserved from ever teaching falsehood in matters of faith (doctrine) and morals. In this self-portrait, the Church does two things: (1) teach with authority and truth, and (2) decide what is true teaching and what is error or heresy.

The Church is not opposed to the constructive criticism of her own theologians, scholars, saints, and reformers, and she even welcomes the help of the so-called secular sciences. But she has the right (because she has the power from Jesus and the Spirit) to make a definitive judgment on whether any of these criticisms, ideas, and reforms are valid or invalid, that is, whether they are in line with true doctrine or expressions of heresy. It is not a matter of mere men (pope, bishops, or both of these in councils) deciding what saving truth is: it is a matter of the authority given to the Church by Jesus and the abiding presence of the Spirit of truth in the Church. The Spirit speaks the truth to the Church through Scripture and through the tradition of the Spirit's abiding presence in the Church from her foundation until the Lord comes again.

Over the years, under the direction of the Holy Spirit, the Catholic Church has known herself to be the original Church of Jesus and she has used the great Church councils to clarify what the truth of Jesus is against wayward, incomplete, or heretical teachings of some of her children. For political or religious reasons, these "breakaway children" (for example, Photius and Luther) established their own versions of the Church. Various Church councils (for instance, Trent in the case of Luther and the sixteenth-century Reformers) condemned their ideas as either contrary to the Spirit-directed Tradition (the constant faith of the Church) or incomplete or unbalanced.

Vatican II has not — and could not — change that. The council, however, has preferred to stress the ideas, teachings, and practices of the churches originating with Photius and Luther that are "Catholic," of the "tradition," and that form a solid basis for an eventual unity (God willing) of all in one Church once again. For the Lord founded one Church, not hundreds with various degrees of contradiction, disunity, and incompleteness among them.

Thus, Vatican Council II restates the Catholic Church's understanding of herself as the original Church not in exclusive language ("The Church of Christ is the Roman Catholic Church") but in what appears to be inclusive language ("The Church of Christ subsists in the Roman Catholic Church")[2] that does not exclude the other Christian churches nor deny "the many elements of sanctification and of truth" that they possess. In a later statement, the council speaks of Roman Catholics as "fully incorporated into the Church."[3] From these statements, one may say that the Catholic Church does not wish to regard the other Christian churches as external to the Church but in varying degrees of membership within the Church, though lacking the fullness of teaching and of sacraments that "full incorporation" in the Church of Christ's foundation requires.

On our second point: What Vatican II does *not* say about the other Christian churches (Protestant) may be inferred from what it says about the Eastern Orthodox churches. These Eastern forms of Christianity hold a "special position" relative to the Catholic Church because of their ancient "origin, their situation as fully constituted churches," and in that they "belong to the full catholic and apostolic character of the Church."[4]

In other words, short of a few important items, these churches reflect most of what constitutes the Catholic Church as to doctrine, authority, and sacraments. Then, as has been noted, "the Decree on Ecumenism is more guarded in its exposition of the ecclesial reality, faith and structures of the separated churches . . . in the West ['Protestant' churches], which have arisen as a result of the Reformation in the 16th century."[5]

Previous councils (especially Trent and Vatican I) are quite clear on the fact that the Roman Catholic Church is the original, ancient Church of the Lord's foundation. In those days, the Eastern Orthodox churches were considered to be basically schismatic (that is, denying no major doctrine and lacking no major component of Catholic fullness but separated from the unity of Catholicism). The Reformation (Protestant) churches, however, were seen to be truly lacking and heretical. They based themselves on their own interpretations of Scripture rather than on the authoritative interpretation of the Catholic Church. They, generally, reduced the number of sacraments to two instead of Catholicism's seven.

In addition, they rejected among other things the sacrificial nature of the Mass, the divinely established authority of bishops, the reality of the Lord's presence at the Eucharist, and the position of the Holy Father (the bishop of Rome). They devised a different understanding of grace and salvation, of merit and the meaning of good works. They rejected the centuries-old Christian teaching that Mary is not only the Mother of Jesus but the Mother of God. They denied so much of the Catholic tradition (the Christian faith of the prior fifteen hundred years) that they were excommunicated. (We should remember that most of the founders of the Reformation were Catholic priests and deacons, seen by Mother Church as disobedient sons.) Today, most Protestants deny moral norms that Catholics believe are of Christ.

Vatican II, in view of the present-day situation that is long removed from those old days of "her disobedient sons," has chosen to stress not the heresies of the past but the positive and parallel aspects of faith and practice that these Christian churches have with Catholicism. Thus, there is a legitimate sense in which Vatican II can speak of the original Church as "Catholicism," a church that the Roman faith uninterruptedly and fully contains but also a church to which the Eastern Orthodox churches and the Protestant Christian churches of the present-day likewise belong — with varying degrees of Catholic fullness. This is the view of Catholicism that is being presented more and more by contemporary theologians. And it leads to our third point: the call to fullness of faith or the call to ecclesial (church) fullness.

Deeper than the call of ecumenism is the call to live now the fullness of the Church's faith. We should live fully the life of the Church. It cannot be the Lord's will that we live his way by bits and pieces; that we settle for forms of his Church that originate (however gracefully) late in Christian history and are clearly the foundations of men at war with the ancient, Spirit-directed Church of the Lord's foundation. It cannot be the Lord's will that we settle for Scripture alone when Tradition has antecedently settled on Scripture and sacrament. We cannot be comfortable with fifteen hundred confessional churches claiming the guidance of the Lord's Spirit of truth and unity when they so often claim that Spirit's direction on their contradictions of one another. Even if they could be taken all together as a single unit, they stand opposed to the overwhelming majority of Christians (the Roman Catholics and the Eastern Orthodox) who hold, and have held for centuries, as fundamental the doctrines and practices rejected by the Reformation churches.

Jesus says in John 10:10, "I have come so that they may have life and have it to the full" (*Jerusalem Bible*). Some Christians may say that they are happy with the personal faith they have, perhaps a faith based on simple trust in Jesus or one based on their own felt experience of the Spirit moving them. None of this is more than a steppingstone to the Church as "Christ's sacrament of encounter with man."[6] Many will say (as the Catholic Church affirms) that salvation and grace are possible outside of unity with the Church. However, such is not the Lord's desire, he who identified himself with his Church. The way of the Church is the Lord's way. Why do many people still keep insisting on "my way" and "my" version of Church as if the Church were of their foundation rather than the Lord's? The Church cannot be reduced to anyone's private, individualistic mode of walking in the way of the Lord.

The fullness that is defined by the term "Catholic" means that I cannot settle for reductionism — of doctrine, practice, Bible interpretation, range of sacraments, and the instruments by which the Lord mediates his saving grace to me. I cannot settle for the constraints and reductions of each new reformer (there will be reformers until the end of time) in history, for even the Reformation changes were immediately subjected to additional reforms themselves. Whatever may be the contribution of the reforming mind in Church history, fullness of doctrine and grace has never been its characteristic. To me, this is one of the crucial issues in Christian history.

The fourth point is the right of the Dr. Johns of the world to seek admission (and a warm welcome) into the fullness of the faith, into Catholicism, if that is where their conscience leads them. This is such a basic matter — a right mentioned expressly in the "Decree on Ecumenism" and the subject of another decree, the "Decree on Religious Liberty." A fundamental principle of Catholic ethics is the obligation we have to form our conscience, follow it, and take responsibility for it. One wonders how some priests and religion teachers today can misplace so elementary an ethical principle when it comes to people seeking union with the Catholic Church. One wonders, too, why the same priests and religion teachers are vocal on ecumenism and silent on convert ministry. We should not exalt the Catholic Church triumphantly and imperially. But neither should we shortchange her as the ordinary, divinely willed, Spirit-directed means of union with the Lord.

She has received into her fold seekers as far back as St. Augustine and as recent as Dr. John. She has been there — alone — throughout the entirety of Christian history. Who else can make the claim?

In my files is a letter from Dr. John, written the evening of his reception into the Catholic Church. It reads simply: "Thank you for the joy of this day. And thanks especially for reminding me that like Newman [the convert cardinal] I have moved from faith to faith; that I have not abandoned my cherished heritage but found its fullness."

ENDNOTES

1. See "Dogmatic Constitution on the Church," *Vatican Council II* (Collegeville, Minn.: Liturgical Press, 1984), Vol. 1, p. 357.
2. Ibid.
3. Ibid., p. 366.
4. *The Christian Faith*, ed. by J. Neuner and J. Dupuis (New York: Alba House, 1982), p. 262. Also "Decree on Ecumenism," *Vatican Council II*, pp. 464-467.
5. *The Christian Faith*, p. 262.
6. See "Dogmatic Constitution on the Church," in op. cit., p. 350.

TELL ME WHY I SHOULD BE A CATHOLIC WHEN...

the moral teachings of the Church seem so strict — can't we be good Christians by following our own consciences?

This is a question asked not only by non-Catholics but by many within the Catholic Church. Among these some would disagree completely with Church teachings about such matters as sex outside of marriage, avoidance of luxury, or the sacredness of life from womb to tomb to eternity. Others accept our basic morality but want to see specific ethical concepts more as guidelines than as norms.

Is it not the right of a mature Christian to make free moral decisions in his or her own case? Such choice should reflect Scripture and tradition but ultimately manifest the believer's own personal standards — a matter not of tight legal injunctions but of inner conscience.

There is much to be found in Catholic teaching that would appear to allow for approaching moral decisions on an individual basis. In *Vatican Council II* we find these words: "It is through his conscience that man sees and recognizes the demands of the divine law. He is bound to follow this conscience faithfully in all his activity so that he may come to

God, who is his last end. Therefore he must not be forced to act contrary to his conscience" ("Declaration on Religious Liberty," No. 3).

The council also explains: "Deep within his conscience man discovers a law which he has not laid upon himself but which he must obey. Its voice, ever calling him to love and do what is good and to avoid evil, tells him inwardly at the right moment: do this, shun that. For man has in his heart a law inscribed by God. His dignity lies in observing this law, and by it he will be judged. His conscience is man's most secret core, and his sanctuary" ("Pastoral Constitution on the Church in the Modern World," No. 16).

Faced with hard choices in areas such as mercy killing, remarriage after divorce involving a valid marriage, contraception, homosexual activity, or engaging as a combatant in a war the justice of which is questionable, many people — whatever their philosophy or religion — will want to avoid fixed structures in favor of their own judgment of personal conscience.

Catholics caught in such dilemmas may consider "bending the rules" to "resolve" the dilemmas and make them acceptable on the basis of the apparent changes in Church teaching over the years on questions such as slavery, usury, or the meaning of sex in marriage.

Noticing from reading the newspapers and magazines that even some Catholic theologians disagree about certain moral issues may also suggest the necessity of making up one's mind oneself. Behavior that seems contradictory to Scripture or tradition will often be challenged by other Christians with questions such as: "The Bible condemns premarital sex as fornication, so how can you justify it?" or "How can you go to Holy Communion each week when you are living with someone you are not married to?"

Such rebukes will sometimes receive a response such as this: "Jesus was merciful to sinners — where do you get off being so legalistic and self-righteous?"

And yet the whole idea of individual morality is contrary to a broader view of Scripture and tradition. Absolutizing personal conscience presupposes that all people are innocent and well-intended, eager to sacrifice their own individual needs in obedience to God for the good of others. While it is true that God made us to be good, very soon our first parents chose to disobey without concern for the consequences.

After the fall of Adam and Eve, we all have a tendency to self-deception or what the moral philosopher Dietrich von Hildebrand called "value-blindness." We know with what false reasoning slave traders rationalized their evil deeds. To justify their greed, slave traders convinced themselves that slaves were not real persons or that they were such children they could not live without masters.

We find similar forms of value-blindness in our times whereby abortionists persuade themselves that a baby in the womb is not a real person.

In the Book of Proverbs (16:25) it is written, "Sometimes there is a way that seems to be right, but in the end it is the way to death."

Dramatic examples of value-blindness undermining conscience to be found in Scripture are David's adultery with Bathsheba and his plot to kill her husband. In the New Testament, does not Caiaphas argue that the death of Jesus is justified for "the good of the people"? The status of the Jewish political leaders as friends of the Romans was not to be displaced by a Messiah-King.

A thoughtful reading of the Bible bears out the necessity of moral authority for less-than-perfect human creatures. As one speaker put it: it's not the ten suggestions; it's the Ten Commandments!

Does that mean that there is no room for personal conscience? No. When we make choices between two good possibilities such as serving the community as a fire fighter or a doctor, we ought to decide on the basis of personal talents and circumstances.

However, Catholic tradition based on a scriptural understanding of human nature insists on the need for moral norms when it comes to the business of avoiding moral evils. In *The Documents of Vatican II* ("Pastoral Constitution on the Church in the Modern World"), this clarification is given: ". . . when there is a question of harmonizing conjugal love with the responsible transmission of life, the moral aspect of any procedure does not depend solely on sincere intentions or on an evaluation of motives. It must be determined by objective standards" (No. 51).

Respectful dissent from Church moral teaching is not even an accepted category for theologians, according to the "Instruction on the Ecclesial Vocation of the Theologian" (*Origins*, May 14, 1990, IV-B, Nos. 32-41).

John Paul II's encyclical *Veritatis Splendor* (or *The Splendor of Truth*), which came out in 1993, contains these words about how important it is that Christians not only be sincere but that they choose *the good*: "The rational ordering of the human act to the good in its truth and the voluntary pursuit of that good, known by reason, constitute morality. Hence human activity cannot be judged as morally good merely because it is a means for attaining one or another of its goals, or simply because the subject's intention is good. Activity is morally good when it attests to and expresses the voluntary ordering of the person to his ultimate end and the conformity of a concrete action with the human good as it is acknowledged in its truth by reason. If the object of the concrete action is not in harmony with the true good of the person, the choice of that action makes our will and ourselves morally evil, thus putting us in conflict with our ultimate end, the supreme good, God himself" (No. 72).

About false teaching, John Paul II writes: "No damage must be done to the *harmony between faith and life: the unity of the Church* is damaged not only by Christians who reject or distort the truths of faith but also by those who disregard the moral obligations to which they are called by the Gospel (cf. 1 Cor 5:9-13). The Apostles decisively rejected any separation between the commitment of the heart and the actions which express or prove it (cf. 1 Jn 2:3-6). And ever since Apostolic times the Church's Pastors have unambiguously condemned the behaviour of those who fostered division by their teaching or by their actions" (No. 26).

Does that mean that John Paul II has no sympathy for how hard the moral struggle is for Christians of our times? Not at all. He explains his teaching on weakness and mercy: "*Only in the mystery of Christ's Redemption do we discover the 'concrete' possibilities of man.* It would be a very serious error to conclude ... that the Church's teaching is essentially only an 'ideal' which must then be adapted, proportioned, graduated to the so-called concrete possibilities of man, according to a 'balancing of the goods in question.' But what are the 'concrete possibilities of man'? And of *which* man are we speaking? Of man *dominated* by lust or of man *redeemed by Christ*? This is what is at stake: the *reality* of Christ's redemption. *Christ has redeemed us!* This means that he has given us the possibility of realizing *the entire* truth of our being; he has set our freedom free from the *domination* of concupiscence. And if redeemed man still sins, this is not due to an imperfection of Christ's redemptive act, but to man's will not to avail himself of the grace which flows from that act. God's command is of course proportioned to man's capabilities; but to the capabilities of the man to whom the Holy Spirit has been given; of the man who, though he has fallen into sin, can always obtain pardon and enjoy the presence of the Holy Spirit" (No. 103).

"In this context, appropriate allowance is made both for *God's mercy* towards the sinner who converts and for the *understanding of human weakness*. Such understanding never means compromising and falsifying the standard of good and evil in order to adapt it to particular circumstances. It is quite human for the sinner to acknowledge his weakness and to ask mercy for his failings; what is unacceptable is the attitude of one who makes his own weakness the criterion of the truth about the good, so that he can feel self-justified, without even the need to have recourse to God and his mercy. An attitude of this sort corrupts the morality of society as a whole, since it encourages doubt about the objectivity of the moral law in general and a rejection of the absoluteness of moral prohibitions regarding specific human acts, and it ends up by confusing all judgments about values" (No. 104).

But what about so-called changed moral teaching of the past? To respond to this question it is necessary to do some research concerning each moral issue.

Slavery was never considered a good thing by the Catholic Church. As in Scripture, it was tolerated as an alternative to the more cruel practice of killing those captured in war. Slave-trading in later times was condemned by the Church and slavery was outlawed by the Spanish at the urging of the Church in 1530, three hundred thirty-three years before our Emancipation Proclamation. Does that mean no Catholics had slaves? No. Slave-owning was tolerated, not approved, with a view toward the benefits to a slave of being owned by a benevolent person rather than tortured by an evil one. For the slave on the block this seemed to be a better alternative, until liberation was a legal possibility.

Usury (loan-sharking today) was condemned and is still condemned. Usury is basically charging exorbitant interest in order to exploit others. In early times of the Church the practice of giving loans was always exploitative. Later, legitimate banking practices proved that granting loans at small interest could be a benefit to the needy.

If in fact moral teachings in their essence have not changed, does this mean that every Catholic simply renounces his or her conscience and just asks the priest what to do in every aspect of life?

Not really. Although obedience to legitimate authority, called by God to shepherd us, is always right and good, we are also called to ponder God's will in our hearts — to love his law. Jesus is merciful but also firm. "Your sins are forgiven, . . . and from now on do not sin again" (Luke 7:48 and John 8:11).

Here are some scriptural and traditional perspectives on some of the moral teachings of the Church that are deemed most controversial, taken from my book called *Living in Love: About Christian Ethics* (Boston: St. Paul Books and Media).

Social Justice

Central Problem: Minimalism — the idea that Christians can pursue their own individual needs with a minimum of concern for others.

Scripture and Tradition: "Is not this the fast that I choose: to loose the bonds of injustice, to undo the thongs of the yoke, to let the oppressed go free, to break every yoke? Is it not to share your bread with the hungry. . . ?" (Isaiah 58:6-7).

In one particular biblical concordance, there are more than two hundred entries under "just" and "justice" and thousands of others explaining how important it is to care deeply about the needs of the suffering.

Although many disobedient, selfish Catholics have chosen to cling to luxurious lifestyles rather than give generously to the needy or donate time to creating more just societal patterns and laws, Church teaching is clear as to principle: "God destined the earth and all it contains for all men and all peoples so that all created things would be shared fairly by all mankind under the guidance of justice tempered by charity" (*Vatican Council II*, "Pastoral Constitution on the Church in the Modern World," No. 69).

In his encyclical *On the Development of Peoples* Pope Paul VI summarized and applies the constant teaching of the Church in this regard: " 'If someone who has the riches of this world sees his brother in need and closes his heart to him, how does the love of God abide in him?' (1 Jn. 3:17) It is well known how strong were the words used by the Fathers of the Church to describe the proper attitude of persons who possess anything toward persons in need. To quote St. Ambrose: 'You are not making a gift of your possessions to the poor person. You are handing over to him what is his. For what is given in common for the use of all, you have arrogated to yourself. The world is given to all, and not only to the rich.' That is, private property does not constitute for anyone an absolute unconditioned right. No one is justified in keeping for his exclusive use what he does not need, when others lack necessities. In a word, according to the traditional doctrine as found in the Fathers of the Church and the great theologians, the right to property must never be exercised to the detriment of the common good."

This teaching has been confirmed many times in encyclicals about social justice by John Paul II. Each individual Catholic can exercise his or her conscience to determine how to apply such norms to specific responsibilities in the community.

Ethics of War

Main Problem: Because of nationalism and other causes, many Christians fail to see that most wars are unjust and therefore anti-Christian. We should not automatically support any war our country decides to engage in.

Scripture and Tradition: Proclamations about peace are innumerable in the Bible and in Catholic teaching. Jesus continually greets others with the words "Peace be to you." He proclaims that the peacemakers shall be blessed (Matthew 5:9) and he is called the Prince of Peace. On the other hand, the role of being a soldier was not looked down upon, in itself, as evil (see Luke 3.10-14).

In the 1973 U.S. bishops' pastoral letter "The Challenge of Peace," there is a summary of our long tradition of condemning deliberate killing of the innocent. An update, "The Harvest of Justice Is Sown in Peace" (1993), stresses how, now that the threat of nuclear war had diminished, there is special need to underline the traditional teaching that war must be the last resort, not the first; how we must try to eliminate causes of violence and apply sanctions before killing people.

Our tradition also insists that self-defense can be justified under certain conditions.

Here are some of the main points of the tradition called the just-war ethic:

1. Everything should be done to avoid wars.

2. If this is impossible and if our country is not the aggressor, our defense of ourselves or other in-

nocent countries should never involve the use of such improper means as deliberately targeting the innocent. "Any act of war aimed indiscriminately at the destruction of entire cities or of extensive areas along with their population is a crime against God and man himself. It merits unequivocal and unhesitating condemnation" (*The Documents of Vatican II*, "Pastoral Constitution on the Church in the Modern World," No. 80).

3. Wars should not be engaged in or prolonged when there is little hope of victory.

Abortion

Main Problem: Although everyone realizes that abortion is tragic, some think it could be the lesser of two evils in cases of mothers who are too young, too poor, unmarried, or incapable of dealing with a handicapped child or with rape or incest.

Scripture and Tradition: "Whoever sheds the blood of a human, by a human shall that person's blood be shed; for in his own image God made humankind" (Genesis 9:6).

Exodus 23:7 tells us, ". . . do not kill the innocent and those in the right."

"Behold, children are a precious gift of the Lord, the fruit of the womb is a reward" (paraphrase of Psalm 127:3).

Psalm 139:13-16 describes the awesomeness surrounding conception: "For it was you who formed my inward parts; you knit me together in my mother's womb. . . . My frame was not hidden from you, when I was being made in secret, intricately woven in the depths of the earth. Your eyes beheld my unformed substance. In your book were written all the days that were formed for me, when none of them as yet existed."

The Documents of Vatican II warn us: ". . . whatever is opposed to life itself, such as any type of murder, genocide, abortion, euthanasia, or willful self-destruction, whatever violates the integrity of the human person . . . all these things and others of their like are infamies indeed. They poison human society, but they do more harm to those who practice them than those who suffer from the injury. Moreover, they are a supreme dishonor to the Creator" ("Pastoral Constitution on the Church in the Modern World," No. 27).

Compassion and real help for the mother pregnant against her own wishes should be extended generously as well as forgiveness for those who live in great pain repenting an abortion. Such loving attitudes and acts do not invalidate showing love to the baby through adoption, and through efforts to stop abortion by legal means and by nonviolent protest.

Euthanasia

Main Problem: Many people wonder whether the sustaining of life by extraordinary means even in cases involving great suffering or expense is required. In the case of someone in excruciating pain or born with extreme defects, could not a positive act of ending the life of such a person be more charitable than letting that individual live on?

Scripture and Tradition: "Thou shalt not kill" (see, for example, Exodus 20:13 and Luke 18:20, *Douay-Rheims Bible*). The biblical injunction against killing is supported by the very progressive Greek

Hippocratic oath taken by all doctors, "I will neither give a deadly drug to anybody who asks for it, nor will I make a suggestion to this effect."

Direct killing of innocent persons for any reason has always been ruled out in Judeo-Christian morality. (In the case of war it is usually maintained that a person who unjustly kills others forfeits his or her right to life and is certainly not innocent.) Killing an innocent, including oneself, is a way of usurping God's power over creation and death. This doctrine was reiterated by Pope Pius XII during the Nazi times in response to questions of eugenics and genocide.

This doctrine also reflects the religious conviction that every human being is infinitely precious regardless of any consideration of development.

We are creatures who owe our existence to God. We belong to him and we must accept the problems of suffering in our lives that remain even when we try to alleviate them by every pain-killing means available.

On the other hand, the Church teaches that we do not have to use extraordinary means to keep a person alive who is in great pain or causing tremendous burdens. What are extraordinary and what are ordinary means vary from age to age and culture to culture. This makes it difficult to apply some neat, exact measure. However, moral theologians normally say that ordinary means are those commonly accepted, readily available, without extreme difficulty in terms of pain and expense. Heroic measures that offer no reasonable hope of benefit do not have to be used; however, food and water are considered to be not medicine but an ordinary means to keep someone alive even if administered by a feeding tube that does not cause pain.

Divorce

Main Problem: As divorce and remarriage has become more and more acceptable in the society around us, many Christians question whether in some cases it might not be the most loving thing to humbly accept the fact that some marriages cause more pain than joy and some couples seem to be unable to be reconciled with each other. In such cases should not each be free to try to make a better life with someone else? Especially, should the innocent party who has been deserted or maltreated have to live singly for the rest of his or her life?

Scripture and Tradition: "It was also said, 'Whoever divorces his wife, let him give her a certificate of divorce.' But I say to you that anyone who divorces his wife, except on the ground of unchastity [interpreted as referring to a woman found not to be a virgin before marriage during engagement — breaking the engagement was considered under divorce], causes her to commit adultery and whoever marries a divorced woman commits adultery" (Matthew 5:31-32).

Later on in the gospel of Matthew (19:3-9) we are told: "Some Pharisees came to him [Jesus] and to test him they asked, 'Is it lawful for a man to divorce his wife for any cause?' He answered, 'Have you not read that the one who made them at the beginning "made them male and female" and said, "For this reason a man shall leave his father and mother and be joined to his wife, and the two shall become one flesh"? . . . Therefore what God has joined together,

99

let no one separate.' They said to him, 'Why then did Moses command us to give a certificate of dismissal and to divorce her?' He said to them, 'It was because you were so hard-hearted that Moses allowed you to divorce your wives, . . . And I say to you, whoever divorces his wife [or her husband], except for unchastity, and marries another commits adultery."

The emphasis in Catholic tradition is on the importance of fidelity to the valid bond of love undertaken in marriage. Marriages can only be annulled if such a valid bond can be proven never to have existed, as in the case of those forced to marry, those who do not consummate their marriages in sexual intercourse due to sexual impotence, or, in recent times, those who purposely and consciously exclude the notion of marriage as a bond "till death do us part."

Of late, due to a greater knowledge of the effect of certain mental disorders on the freedom of the person, more marriages are being annulled on the basis of extreme immaturity making a free-will decision of self-donation impossible.

A very beautiful summary of Church teaching on divorce is included in the U.S. bishops' pastoral letter of 1976 "To Live in Christ Jesus," from which I now quote:

> Every human being has a need and right to be loved, to have a home where he or she can put down roots and grow. The family is the first and indispensable community in which this need is met. Today, when productivity, prestige or even physical attractiveness are regarded as the gauge of personal worth, the family has a special vocation to be a place

where people are loved not for what they do or what they have but simply because they are.

A family begins when a man and woman publicly proclaim before the community their mutual commitment so that it is possible to speak of them as one body. Christ teaches that God wills the union of man and woman in marriage to be lifelong, a sharing of life for the length of life itself.

The Old Testament takes the love between husband and wife as one of the most powerful symbols of God's love for His people: "I will espouse you to Me forever: I will espouse you in right and in justice, in love and in mercy: I will espouse you in fidelity, and you shall know the Lord." So husband and wife espouse themselves, joined in a holy and loving covenant.

The New Testament continues this imagery: only now the union between husband and wife rises to the likeness of the union between Christ and His Church. Jesus teaches that in marriage men and women are to pledge steadfast unconditional faithfulness which mirrors the faithfulness of the Son of God. Their marriages make this fidelity and love visible to the world. Christ raised marriage in the Lord to the level of a sacrament, whereby this union symbolizes and affects God's special love for the couple in their total domestic and social situation.

Jesus tells us that the Father can and will grant people the greatness of heart to keep such pledges of loving faithfulness. The Church has always believed that in making and keeping noble promises of this sort people can, through the grace of God, grow beyond themselves — grow to the point of being able to love beyond their merely human capacity. Yet contemporary culture makes it difficult for many people to accept this view of marriage. Even some who admire it as an ideal doubt whether it is possible and consider it too risky to attempt. They believe it is better to promise less at the start and so be able to escape from marital tragedy in order to promise once again.

But this outlook itself has increased marital tragedy. Only men and women bold enough to make promises for life, believing that with God's help they can be true to their word as He is to His, have the love and strength to surmount the inevitable challenges of marriage. Such unselfish love, rooted in faith, is ready to forgive when the need arises and to make the sacrifices demanded if something as precious and holy as marriage is to be preserved. For the family to be a place where human beings can grow with security, the love pledged by husband and wife must have as its model the selfless and enduring love of Christ for the Church. "Husbands, love your wives, as Christ loved the Church. He gave himself up for her."

Some say even valid sacramental marriages can deteriorate to such an extent that the marital union dies and the spouses are no longer obliged to keep their promise of lifelong fidelity. Some even urge the Church to acknowledge such dissolution and allow the parties to enter new, more promising unions. We reject this view. In reality it amounts to a proposal to forego Christian marriage at the outset and substitute something entirely different. It would weaken marriage further, by paying too little heed to Jesus' call to identify ourselves with His redeeming love, which endures all things. Its fundamental difficulty is that it cannot be reconciled with the Church's mission to be faithful to the word entrusted to it. The covenant between a man and woman joined in Christian marriage is as indissoluble and irrevocable as God's love for His people and Christ's love for His Church.

We must seek ways by which the Church can mediate Christ's compassion to those who have suffered marital tragedy, but at the same time we may do nothing to undermine His teaching concerning the beauty and meaning of marriage and in particular His prophetic demands concerning the indissolubility of the unions of those who marry in the Lord. The Church must ever be faithful to the command to serve the truth in love.

[The practice of some couples in second marriages to receive Communion without an annulment is not allowable except with permission in some cases where evidence of the nullity of the previous marriages is unobtainable as, for instance, in the case of documents destroyed in wartime.]

Premarital and Extramarital Sex

Main Problem: Given the tremendous emphasis on pleasure in contemporary society, it is very difficult for people to impose restraints on themselves. Also, since many think that marriages should not be entered into before the age of twenty-one or even later, it is thought to be too difficult to restrain sexual needs until that time. Although most Christians reject free love, some think that in the case of an engaged couple who have to wait a long time for marriage, premarital intercourse could be permitted. Others think that in the case of marriages involving great difficulties, extramarital sex might be licit.

Scripture and Tradition: The scriptural word for premarital sex is "fornication," and for extramarital sex "adultery." Some claim that these matters are not emphasized in Scripture because they do not realize what these terms refer to. There are many references in Scripture to the forbidding of any form of fornication or adultery — see especially the commandment "Neither shall you covet your neighbor's wife" (Deuteronomy 5:21); refer also, for example, to Matthew 5:27-30, Hebrews 13:4, and 1 Corinthians 6:9, 18.

Tradition has been very strong on these two temptations. Contrary to some opinions, these teachings have in no way been changed in recent years. They are reaffirmed in authoritative documents to the present.

Using another person for sexual pleasure violates that individual's dignity. Those who engage in recreational sex are value-blind to the deep meaning of this sphere, destined as it is to express the total self-donation of marriage and to be open to the procreation of a new human person — the baby.

But what if the motive is not lust but real love? Real love seeks commitment, not an open-ended affair. Great intimacy without the marriage bond leads to the devastating wound of rejection and also the tragic desire to get rid of any children whose conception occurs in spite of ineffective contraception.

Church history is full of examples of happy, holy, chaste people who did not think having sexual intimacy was a necessity, beginning with Jesus, Mary, and Joseph.

Contraception

Main Problem: Due to the great difficulty of raising families in cities, the problem of poverty, and many other obstacles, many couples think it unwise to have large families. Of these many are unacquainted with the natural rhythms of the woman's fertile cycle, which when properly understood requires only a minimum of abstinence from sexual intercourse to avoid an untimely pregnancy. This state of affairs has made artificial contraception more and more attractive as an alternative for many Christian couples.

Scripture and Tradition: Throughout history many different methods of preventing birth have been used, including the use of drugs and magic, or sorcery (see, for instance, Galatians 5:20 and Revelation 21:8, 22:15). Throughout history the Church has condemned such practices over and over again, culminating in Pope Paul VI's encyclical *Humanae Vitae* in 1968. Since then, attention has also been paid to the added grave immorality of those pills, IUD's (intrauterine devices), and the like that really abort the already fertilized egg. It is Catholic teaching that human life begins when the sperm meets the egg.

Not too long ago all Christian churches agreed with the Catholic position on contraceptives. It was understood that fertility was a gift of God, even if a burden, just as is all of life on earth.

In Catholic teaching through the centuries the emphasis has been on our call to use the gifts God has given us in ways that do not violate their God-given nature. I should use my voice to tell truth, not abuse its communicative nature by telling lies. I should use my reproductive organs in a life-giving way, not abuse them by sterilization, or by blocking the sperm and egg from reaching each other, or by distorting a woman's entire system with contraceptive pills. One can think of the fertile time of a woman's cycle as a sacred time. A woman should be proud that she has this gift rather than violating that time. Natural family planning sets the gift aside by not using it, whereas contraceptives use that time while abusing it.

Does that mean couples should have one baby after another no matter what their circumstances? No. Not any more than a person need talk incessantly. We can remain silent when speech would be hurtful — as do those who refuse to reveal the whereabouts of persons searched for by criminals or by tyrants who intend to kill them. In a similar way we can decide not to use the fertile time in a woman's cycle — only a few days — during times when serious reasons make it better to postpone the coming of a new baby. The new methods of natural family planning are easy and when used carefully have a much higher rate of effectiveness than most unnatural methods.

Many Catholic theologians who originally dissented from magisterial teaching on this subject have come to see how dreadful are the effects of the contraceptive culture on young people as well as on married ones. It is clear that the use of contraceptives gives people a false sense of security in pursuing sex outside of marriage and adulterous sex. A contraceptive failure often leads to the aborting of the child.

For more information on this subject see *The Art*

of Natural Family Planning by John and Sheila Kippley (Cincinnati: The Couple to Couple League, 1989).

Homosexuality

Main Problem: In recent years due to causes psychological, sociological, and moral, there has been an enormous increase in open homosexuality. Moreover, there is agitation among homosexuals who consider themselves to be Christians that their lifestyle be accepted as an alternative one rather than condemned as intrinsically evil.

Scripture and Tradition: Scripture refers to homosexuality, masturbation, and fornication with animals, etc., as unnatural and unclean acts. Passages can be found condemning them in Genesis 19:5 (note that in Scripture "to know" in a sexual context means intercourse); Leviticus 18 and 20:13; Judges 19:22; Wisdom 14:22-29; Ephesians 4:19. And the most oft-quoted — Romans 1:26-28, 32 — tells us:

> For this reason God gave them up to degrading passions. Their women exchanged natural intercourse for unnatural, and in the same way also the men, giving up natural intercourse with women, were consumed with passion for one another. Men committed shameless acts with men and received in their own persons the due penalty for their error.
>
> And since they did not see fit to acknowledge God, God gave them up to a debased mind and to things that should not be done. . . . They know God's decree, that those who practice such things deserve to die [that is, a spiritual death] — yet they not only do them but even applaud others who practice them.

The wrongness of homosexual practices has been reaffirmed over and over again through the present day in the Catholic tradition. For a refutation of arguments given to justify it see John Harvey's *Homosexuality: A Pastoral Approach* (San Francisco: Ignatius Press). This book also discusses psychological causes as well as successful pastoral group support encouraging a holy, chaste lifestyle. For a psychologist's approach see Joseph Nicolosi's *Reparative Therapy for the Homosexual* (Northvale, N.J.: Jason Aronson, Inc.).

Having a homosexual orientation as opposed to practice is not in itself blameworthy, since many times it is rooted in psychological disorders. Growth in Christian maturity makes it possible to control such desires, and intense counseling may lead to healing of psychological problems, especially if the person involved wants to change. As Pope Paul VI states: "The Master, who speaks with great severity in this matter [of chastity] (Mt. 5:28), does not propose an impossible thing. We Christians, regenerated in baptism, though we are not freed from this kind of weakness, are given the grace to overcome it" ("To Live the Paschal Mystery," May 1971).

Many are the men and women who once thought the Church's teachings on morality were too strict but who later went on to embrace them, finally viewing them not as a prison but as liberation. Some famous ones are: Augustine, St. Ignatius Loyola, St. Francis of Assisi, Blessed Angela of Foligno, St. Margaret of Cortona, Charles de Foucauld, Malcolm Muggeridge, and Dorothy Day.

TELL ME WHY I SHOULD BE A CATHOLIC WHEN...

the Church is not Bible-based?

This charge — that the Catholic Church is not based on the Bible — is often made by Fundamentalists.[1] They sometimes level it against mainline Protestant churches, too. They bring up old accusations against the Catholic Church that have been discredited long ago as fabrications. They also "set up" Catholic teachings that are not Catholic at all and then proceed to show how these are not Bible-based. Because this game is recognized by self-respecting Catholics and Protestants, the Fundamentalists studiously avoid two things: (1) critical Bible scholarship, and (2) the interfaith dialogue (ecumenism).

Nevertheless, millions of Americans flock to the Fundamentalists. These Americans are not just folksy Bible-belt believers. There are also urbanites, disenchanted with mainline Christianity. They want just a "simple," personal, and uncomplicated version of Christ's gospel. They find it in Fundamentalism.

Our task here is to face the charge that the Catholic Church does not base herself on the Bible but on "the traditions of men." This charge follows from the fact that the Catholic Church does pay great attention to what she calls "sacred Tradition." Sacred Tradition is the development of doctrine and practice in the Church for the past two thousand years, under the direction of the Holy Spirit that was first given to the Church at Pentecost. This "sacred Tradition" has nothing to do with other "traditions" that come and go in the history of the Church and are based in the ethnic, cultural, or devotional life of the Church's many peoples.

If Fundamentalists would only spend a few days observing a Catholic seminary at work, or sit in on a few sessions of the Catholic-Lutheran dialogue, or read the documents of the Second Vatican Council, or quietly study the two-thousand-year-old history of the Catholic Church, they would be quite amazed at the centrality of the Bible in Catholic doctrine, liturgy, study, and life formation. For example, the Catholic Church teaches that the Bible is "written under the inspiration of the Holy Spirit" and that it has God as its author and that it is "handed on as such to the church." This is not the language of a church that does not base itself on the Bible.[2]

The Catholic Church teaches what we are to do with this Bible, or word of God. It "must be acknowledged as teaching firmly, faithfully and without error that truth which God wanted put into the sacred writings for the sake of our salvation." Not only is "easy access" to be available to all Catholics to the Scriptures, care must be taken over translations so that they faithfully give the word of God. All theology must "rest on the written word of God." The clergy and catechists must "hold fast to the sacred scriptures through diligent sacred reading and careful study." Preaching the word and teaching it is "a ministry" of the Church. It is in Scripture more than anywhere else that the sons and daughters of the

Catholic Church find the "excelling knowledge of Jesus Christ."

The Catholic Church does not put "traditions of men" ahead of the Bible. Many Christians, including many Fundamentalists, seem to have the view that God the Father or his Son, Jesus, just handed a Bible to the apostles and said, "There you are — the word of God!" The Bible comes out of the Church's experience under the living Spirit. It existed long before the Reformation happened or Fundamentalism was even thought of. Now since the Bible is the word of God written under divine inspiration by men, how was it put together? And who decided that it is the word of God? And what should it contain? There was no New Testament of the Bible (the key part!) in the time of the Lord or during the first generation of Christians. Then the succeeding generations of Christians had a problem — dozens of written letters (epistles), gospels (for example, the gospel of Thomas), and instructions floating around the Church congregations. Arguments abounded as to what authority or worth all these documents had. Gradually, the Catholic Church decided which were true and which were not, and which would enter the canon (rule) of Scripture and which would be excluded.[3]

How did the Catholic Church come to her decision? She examined the intrinsic worth of each document, and she called on her authority as the Church of the Lord's foundation. In other words, the Church used what the Fundamentalists call a "tradition of men," that is, she claims the power to decide with divine authority what is and what is not the truth of Christ, in this case what is and what is not Sacred Scripture. And this claim is based on the sending of the Holy Spirit of truth upon the Church at Pentecost — centuries before Fundamentalism appeared on the scene! The canon of Scripture — that is, the Bible and its contents — was not determined until the list of St. Athanasius in A.D. 367. That list was accepted by the Church in her proclamation, catechesis, and liturgy. That same Catholic Church has reaffirmed the rule (or canon) of the Bible many times in history. The irony in all of this is the debt Fundamentalists owe Catholicism for the very Scriptures they hold in their hands. Such works — collecting, collating, deciding the canon of Scripture, declaring it God's divine word, reaffirming its importance, preserving it through the Dark Ages, etc. — are an expression of the sacred Tradition that Catholics cherish and Fundamentalists cannot seem to understand.

Down through the centuries the Catholic Church continued to promote the word of God and use it in liturgy and teaching. When people were not able to read, she painted the key Old Testament and New Testament writings in stained glass and in oils for them. She even carved out those same stories and teachings for the people in such things as statues, panels, and bronze church doors, and cut stone exteriors and interiors, displaying them on banners and dramatizing them in the famous miracle and mystery plays. When Europe (that is, most of the Christian world) was overrun by the vandals of the Dark Ages, the Bible was preserved by the love and care (and immense labor) of the scribe-monks. Later, these handwritten and beautifully ornamented Bibles were so treasured (and so few) that princes and lords even tried to steal them. (This is why they were chained and locked — a fact twisted by bigots to misrepresent the Church as "chaining up" the word of God!)

None of this illustrates the Catholic Church as rejecting the Bible and following instead "the traditions of men." Far from it. There is not a single European historian who has not attributed the survival of the Bible (and, indeed, of the Christian faith) to the monks of the Dark Ages, particularly the Irish.

The Catholic Church is aware that she is subject to the rule of faith in the Bible. She has done more than anyone else in history for the Bible. But she is also aware that the Lord promised her, through the foundation of the apostles, "the Holy Spirit . . . [to] teach you everything" (John 14:26) and that the Holy Spirit, or Spirit of truth, descended on her at Pentecost. This abiding presence of the Spirit of truth in the Church and directing the Church since Pentecost is what she calls "sacred Tradition."

It has inspired the Church to write and canonize the Scripture on the one hand and explain its meaning — authentically and surely — on the other. It is this second aspect that authorizes the Church to say what an unclear line of Scripture truly means. And it is that clarification (not found in the Bible itself) that Fundamentalists label another "tradition of men."

Christians are scandalously divided on what the Bible teaches on key issues such as salvation, grace, infant and adult baptism, the Eucharist, the scope of the gospel, the personal and/or political implications for our living of the kingdom teachings, whether the Bible teaches a social gospel and theology, and the Church as a visible or a hidden fellowship. Such questions are not answered by preachers' conflicting opinions or by a facile reference to "what God told me last night in prayer." There is too much contradiction among the preachers and the televangelists for that. The authoritative interpretations of the Church whose history begins in the apostolic days are the very clarifications Scripture needs, and the very points that the Fundamentalists call "the traditions of men."

Let us see some specific examples of why an authoritative interpretation of Scripture is needed. How is one saved — as Fundamentalists put it? They will answer, "Accept Christ as your personal Savior!" Or you may be told that you must undergo a "baptism of the Holy Spirit." Or, "You must believe in your heart and confess on your lips" the lordship of Jesus (see Romans 10:10). All of these replies have a scriptural foundation and all relate in some way to salvation by faith.

Many of us may have seen "salvation" happen on Fundamentalist TV shows. No doubt people do have some strong emotional experience — and a sense of being saved, maybe a conviction of being saved. But we have received into the Catholic Church over the years men and women who at an earlier time in their lives responded to an altar call at a Billy Graham Crusade or made a commitment to Jesus while experiencing great inner healing at a Pentecostal prayer meeting. We never questioned their sincerity nor would we deny that something of God touched them. But was it salvation? Or was it a special grace on the road to salvation?

What is troubling to us and to the Church in general (not to mention Bible scholars) is the Fundamentalists' simplistic manner of selecting only those texts relating to redemption and salvation that fit a "salvation by faith alone" and that underpin "a conviction of the Holy Ghost that I am saved." This is called "proof-texting." It can be an abuse of Scripture. Have you ever heard a Fundamentalist respond to the scholar who says: "The Bible does not teach salvation or justification by faith alone"? Have you ever seen a Fundamentalist interpret Paul's admonition to the Philippian believers: ". . . beloved, . . . work out your own salvation with fear and trembling" (Philippians 2:12)? Or his stark admission to his convert Corinthians (which applies to them, too): "I punish my body . . . so that after proclaiming to others I myself should not be disqualified" (1 Corinthians 9:27)? Or the remarkable warning of Jesus to his followers: "Not everyone who says to me, 'Lord, Lord,' will enter the kingdom of heaven, but only the one who does the will of my Father in heaven" (Matthew 7:21)? What are these texts saying in relation to salvation by faith alone? They are saying that one must cooperate with grace in order to be saved and in order to stay in the way of salvation. And this lifelong cooperation on my part with grace represents the "works" that Fundamentalists indict Catholics for and regard as a lessening of the deed of Christ and an attack upon the gifts that faith and salvation are.

Abraham was "justified" through his faith in God (see Romans 4:3), yet he never believed in Jesus in his heart or confessed him on his lips. In fact, no one in the long history of God's people of Israel up to the time of Christ ever even heard of Jesus. And yet it is clear from the Bible that many were "saved" in ages past. The overwhelming majority of humans who ever lived never even heard of Jesus. Are we to say that perhaps 99.9 percent of the human family ("made in the image and likeness of God") up to the present day have not been "saved"? That's the meaning of the Fundamentalists' interpretation of the text in question.

And what does that interpretation say in regard to two crucial biblical doctrines: (1) that Jesus is the Redeemer of the world (the effective and universally awaited Messiah), and (2) that God is a loving, concerned, caring, and providential Father? And what does it say to the severely mentally handicapped of all the nations: that they cannot be "saved"? What does it say to Nicodemus who was told very clearly by Jesus: ". . . no one can enter the kingdom of God without being born of water and Spirit" (John 3:5)? What does it say to the early generations of Christians (the so-called golden age of belief) who regarded the Jewish babies who were killed by Herod as Christian martyrs and saints? What does it say by way of contrast to St. Paul's "[You Christians must] work out your own salvation with fear and trembling" (Philippians 2:12)? What does it say in the light of the Lord's own powerful view of judgment (salvation) on the last day: "I was hungry and you gave me food; therefore, come and inherit the kingdom. Those of you who saw me hungry and gave me no food, depart from me into eternal darkness" (paraphrase of Matthew 25:34ff)? And what about his words of warning: "Not everyone who says to me, 'Lord! Lord,' will enter the kingdom of heaven, but only the one who does the will of my father. . ." (Matthew 7:21)?

Fundamentalists propose that one is "saved by faith" (to which they add the word "alone"). There are, indeed, any number of New Testament texts stressing the role of faith and grace in the saving process. But Scripture does not teach a salvation by faith alone. Nor does it free me of the need of my cooperation with grace in the gift of my salvation through faith in Jesus. Without saying it in so many words, the main themes of the Bible have certain presuppositions. One of these most crucial presuppositions (or assumptions) is the fact that I cannot be saved without my cooperation with grace.

St. Augustine (and the Catholic Church's Council of Trent) insists that grace requires my cooperation, that salvation depends on my radical and free response. Fundamentalists so emphasize the role of grace (and so minimize the human role) that the God they unwittingly project is a despot — and man a mere robot. God respects us. After all, he made us in his own image and likeness! He does not treat his beloved children like stones! Catholics hold that no one can be saved except by grace, that grace is paramount, but that it is also ineffectual or powerless in the soul that refuses in its radical human freedom to respond to that grace.

The Fundamentalist stresses the need of a baptism of the Holy Spirit. No water baptisms occur on television! But the Bible quotes Jesus saying to Nicodemus: ". . . unless a man be born again of water and the Holy Ghost, he cannot enter into the kingdom of God" (John 3:5, *Douay-Rheims Bible*).

117

It is said that there are now fifteen hundred distinct forms of Christianity in the United States alone. It would be nice to think that despite this plurality at least they all agreed in fundamentals of faith, worship, doctrine, and morals. Such, alas, is not the fact. This appalling scandal (in a religion that was born from the heart of the Lord who prayed for the unity of his Church on his final night on earth and who sent upon that Church the Spirit of unity at Pentecost) is proof enough of the utter need of authoritative interpretation of Scripture. It is from the experience of the Church that the New Testament Scripture was born. It is to that Church that authoritative interpretation of its meaning must be allowed.

In the first part of this chapter we looked at Vatican II's teaching on Scripture in the life of the Church. Then we gave illustrations of Scripture "proof-texting" and its dangers. We spoke of the formation of Scripture in the Church long before the Reformation or the advent of Fundamentalism. But the Fundamentalist will still ask: "Where in Scripture are Catholic teachings such as personal merit, purgatory, infallibility of the pope, use of relics, and the intercessory role of Mary?" The answer is that some are spoken of in part while others are merely shadowed, or implied.

What concerns us more than anything is the theological attitude behind this assumption that sees the Bible as the sole judge of Church meaning and life. The Bible is the word of God: it is not the totality of Christian life and grace. The Protestant Reformers of the sixteenth century thought that relying solely on one rule of faith (the Bible) would simplify things. It has not, and for at least two crucial reasons: (1) the debate over its authentic interpretation, and (2) the issue of reductionism in Christianity, that is, reducing Church life and doctrine and morality to what is "clearly" in the Bible. Jesus never made such a claim for Scripture. Jesus never commissioned a book, not even a New Testament one. He did, however, commission and send the Spirit of truth (and infallibility) on the Church. If we are going to "reduce" everything to "what is clearly in the Bible," then we are in trouble. The fifteen hundred distinct forms of Christianity in the U.S., all claiming to be Bible-based, attest to that!

Christians today tear the Bible apart on both sides of the abortion-choice debate; on both sides of the homosexuality-sin debate; quoting it for and against divorce, premarital sex, nuclear weapons, the death penalty; using it to support and not support (or even actively condemn) the integration of neighborhoods; taking rigid stands for and against the social gospel, water and/or Spirit baptism, Pentecostalism, confirmation in faith, Eucharist, priesthood, inerrancy, meaning of inspiration, faith, gift, grace, and salvation. We could go on for pages.

Yet the Bible is crucial to the Church. The Church stands under the word of God and its rule. But the Church is crucial to the Bible, too. As today's Christian doctrinal chaos and yesterday's tattered Christian history show, the Bible needs the Church as its authentic and Spirit-directed interpreter on many of its themes, concerns, and texts.

Yes, the Church is Bible-based. And she emphatically needs the Bible. More cogent, ironically, is what Fundamentalists do not appreciate, namely the degree to which the Bible needs the Church.

ENDNOTES

1. Fundamentalism was the reaction of some Christians in Europe to liberal Protestantism in the last century. American Fundamentalism today is varied. Its most outspoken branch is characterized by emphasis on "Bible belief," "real Christianity," lack of sacramental and liturgical expression, and a strong anti-Catholic bias.
2. All quotations here are from the "Dogmatic Constitution on Divine Revelation," *Vatican Council II* (Collegeville: Liturgical Press, 1984), Vol. 1, Nos. 11, 22, 24, 25.
3. Karl Rahner and Herbert Vorgrimler, "Canon of Scripture," *Theological Dictionary* (New York: Seabury Press, 1973), p. 65.

TELL ME WHY I SHOULD BE A CATHOLIC WHEN . . .

some Catholic teachings are not Bible-based?

In the previous chapter we addressed the charge that the Catholic Church is not Bible-based. Here, we want to address the Fundamentalists' charge that specific Catholic teachings are not Bible-based.

The basic teachings of the Catholic Church are those of the Old and New Testaments and their unfolding meaning in the life and experience of the Church. The early creedal statements of Christianity remain the form of creed (or profession of what we believe) that we Catholics use at the liturgy on Sundays. There, all of us stand and profess together the Apostles' Creed ("I believe in God. . ."). Most Christians do exactly the same at Sunday church.

If the fundamental creedal statement of the Catholics is the exact same as the fundamental creedal statement of Episcopalians, Anglicans, and mainline Protestantism, what is the point at issue with the Fundamentalists? Why are they so agitated by "false doctrines of Romanism"? Well, a lot of it is ignorance and the biased legacy of history. Some of it is actually due to the overemphasis by Fundamentalists themselves on certain Bible texts and underemphasis on others. Some of it is due to the demand of the Fundamentalists that all doctrines be clearly manifest in the Bible. Some of it is due to the inclusion by Catholics of some books in the canon of Scripture that other versions of the Bible exclude. Some of it is due to the Fundamentalists' own silence in regard to Bible texts that Catholics hold to be important — for example, John 6:48ff on the Eucharist; Matthew 16:13ff on Peter as the rock; John 20:23 on the bestowal of power to forgive men's sins. Nevertheless, let us address the most frequent charges of the Fundamentalists.

Any talk of merit demeans Christ's death.

The Catholic teaching on merit seems to infer that salvation is due to one's own efforts and not to Jesus. It therefore goes against such Bible teaching as: "For by grace you have been saved through faith, and this is not your own doing; it is the gift of God — not the result of works, so that no one may boast" (Ephesians 2:8-9). The Catholic teaching on merit is accused of somehow claiming that Jesus' death was not a full and final atonement for sin. On the contrary, we say that Christ, not we, merited atonement. Only Jesus saves and only the Crucified One merited salvation for us. Nothing we can do of itself can save us or atone for our sins. To Christ alone belongs this glory.

Our merits as distinguished from Christ's saving merit are simply a matter of the value God places on our free cooperation with Jesus so that his blood becomes really efficacious in our regard. It is God who allows us to merit in this sense. Our free cooperation with saving grace is given value by him. St. Augustine (whom Luther called "the doctor of grace") puts it this way: "When God crowns our merits, He crowns His own gifts."[1]

In the New Testament, Jesus tells us that "whoever gives even a cup of cold water to one of these little ones . . . that person will certainly be rewarded" (paraphrase of Matthew 10:42). This text clearly attaches merit to a charitable action. It should be kept carefully in mind that nothing Jesus did (not even Calvary) is effective in human lives without our free cooperation. And that free cooperation with grace is given its own intrinsic merit precisely because God made us free agents, in his own image and likeness, and not dumb animals or robots. The merit of atonement won by Jesus is not lessened by our merit in cooperation; rather, it is made effective in our regard. God eternally chose to respect that cooperation, to look for it, and to reward it. That is what Catholics mean by "our merits." And that is what the Bible means when it teaches through St. Paul: ". . . in my flesh I am completing what is lacking in Christ's afflictions. . ." (Colossians 1:24).

The defense of the uniqueness of Christ's merit does not have to be maintained or defended by silencing, as it were, other biblical teachings such as the providence of God, the necessity of our free cooperation with grace, and all the biblical statements on reward and punishment, good works, and meritorious actions.

Catholics worship Mary.

So the Fundamentalists say. Some Catholics, in genuine ignorance, may do so just as other Christians, in their ignorance, may completely ignore her. The issue is whether the Catholic Church teaches the worship of Mary. The Catholic Church teaches that worship is due to God alone. Worship of Mary (or any human person, place, or thing) is heresy, according to the Church. We do not worship Mary: we accord her a very special honor, or reverence, called veneration. To a lesser degree, we also venerate the heroes of the Christian life. We call them saints.

But Catholics pray to Mary and the saints.

Yes, we Catholics do. But not in the way we pray to God and Jesus and the Spirit. To them we pray in worship: to Mary and the saints we pray in solidarity and intercession. We take our cue from the Bible's account of the wedding feast at Cana. Though Jesus' hour of self-disclosure and public ministry had not yet arrived, he works his first recorded miracle at the intercession of his Mother who wishes to save the young couple from embarrassment on the happiest day of their lives. In response to Mary's request, Jesus changed water into "the good [that is, the choice] wine" (John 2:10). Would he do less for us now at her intercession?

Catholics call Mary ever-virgin, but the Bible says that Jesus had brothers and sisters (see Mark 3:31ff, Luke 8:19ff, and John 7:5).

The above texts make reference to the sisters and brothers of Jesus. But are they referring to natural brothers and sisters, or spiritual brothers and sisters, or cousins of some kind? The answer is not as obviously clear as Fundamentalists assume. For the Bible also records Jesus' saying: "My mother and my brothers are those who hear the word of God and do it" (Luke 8:21). The Bible also records the words of Jesus to Mary and to the apostle John (who had no natural relationship with Jesus): "Woman, here is your son; son, here is your mother" (paraphrase of John 19:26).

The Bible records many instances where people who are clearly unrelated to each other naturally are called "brothers and sisters" of one another. Was it not from the Bible that priests and preachers learned to address their congregations as "dear brothers and sisters"? As a point of historical interest, the overwhelming majority of Christians are members of the Catholic and Orthodox Churches. What do they say in the matter?

The Catholic tradition interprets the "brothers and sisters" of Jesus as cousins, following the widespread mid-Oriental use of the phrase. An Orthodox tradition regards the "brothers and sisters" of Jesus as half-brothers and half-sisters through a prior marriage of (the widower) Joseph, since Orthodox Christians believe in Mary as ever-virgin. We have to say bluntly that the Fundamentalist view of natural brothers and sisters has no support from the early Church either. The interchanging of "brother" and "sister" with "cousin" is widespread in the culture of the Old and New Testaments as well as in the Scriptures themselves. As Karl Keating points out: "Neither Hebrew nor Aramaic, the language spoken by Christ and his disciples, had a special word meaning cousin."[2] Hence, the interchangeability of terms of relationship in the Bible.

Catholics believe that Mary is not just the Mother of Jesus but also the Mother of God.

Yes, they do. And so do the Orthodox churches. And so must any thinking Christian who really believes that Jesus was divine. If he was not divine, then, of course, in no way can Mary be the Mother of God. But some of us (Catholics and Orthodox at least) really do believe in the true and full divinity of Jesus and, quite logically in consequence, in the divine motherhood of Mary. It's as simple as that.

But the Bible does not say directly, "Mary is the Mother of God." Neither does Jesus ever say directly in the Bible (what I hope we all believe), "I am God." Every truth is not contained clearly and directly in the Bible. Many truths have to be inferred. If we accept the full divinity of Jesus, we cannot then do theological gymnastics by pretending that Mary is the mother of the "human" Jesus but is not the mother of the "divine" Jesus. Jesus is two natures in one Person. Mary is not the mother of a nature: there is no such human phenomenon. She is the mother of a whole Person called Jesus. And that Person is the Word made flesh (see John 1:14). Too much, you say? Well, it's Bible-based.

But Catholics call Mary the mediatrix of grace.

When the Bible says that in Jesus we have a mediator with the Father, does that exclude everyone else from having any kind of mediation role in the Church? Is Jesus so exclusively "mediator of a new covenant" (Hebrews 9:15) that all other mediators of grace are a challenge to his uniqueness? The Bible's answer is: Of course not! Salvation and grace are mediated through many instrumentalities — through preacher and word, through conversion and baptism, through confirmation in faith and shepherding, through Eucharist and healing, and through a whole (Bible-named) series of offices, charisms, sacraments, and functions in Church, in "the body of Christ" (1 Corinthians 12:27).

Our ancestors in the faith firmly believed in the intercessory power of Mary and the saints in heaven. Through them as well as through the forms of mediation mentioned above, the infinite graces won by Jesus on Calvary are applied to us. Just as a priest assisted me by baptizing me, or a minister assisted me by celebrating my marriage, or the Church assisted me by training my child in the faith (yet all of these are God's grace), so the Church teaches that we may safely rely on the assistance of Mary and the saints when we invoke their intercession. Why would she who interceded for a young Jewish couple not intercede for me who am represented at the foot of the Cross by St. John, and to whom Jesus addresses the words "Here is your mother" (John 19:27)?

The opinion of the first great scholar-commentator of the Bible, St. Jerome, is worth noting: "If apostles while still in the flesh . . . can pray for others, how much more will they pray for others after they have won their crowns? . . . Shall St. Paul close his lips after death [he who prayed ceaselessly for others] and not utter a syllable for those [who came to faith through him]?"[3]

Yes, Jesus' mediatorship is unique and no one should question that. But it does not negate the intercessory value of Mary and the saints, which has been powerful in the lives of exemplary Christians throughout the generations. Mary's mediation is that of a transmitter. To use an analogy: I give my child a Christmas gift that my wife places under the tree for me. My wife does not thereby become the giver of the gift. She is merely the transmitter, the mediatrix of it.

Only God is infallible — how can the pope be?

Few Protestant or other Christian leaders who are involved in the ecumenical movement today, and in the search for Christian unity, deny that the pope is Peter's successor in the line of what is called "apostolic succession." However, the question of his infallibility raises trouble for many. It may be denied by some mainly because it is unclear and misunderstood.[4] Most people we have received into communion with the Catholic Church got some strange ideas about the pope and the gift of infallibility from parents and preachers in the past.

Infallibility is the grace given the successor of Peter not to make an error in doctrine when he declares a particular Church belief to be binding doctrine. No pope invents new doctrines. For example, we are aware of only one exercise of the Holy Father's infallibility in the twentieth century, namely the teaching of the assumption of Mary into heaven at the end of her earthly life. This centuries-old belief of the Church was formally declared by the pope to be a doctrine of the Church. Pius XII made this solemn pronouncement on November 1, 1950, after consulting his brother bishops of the world and receiving their confirmation. So it was not a new belief but one held firmly throughout the Christian centuries, East and West.

Infallibility is a grace belonging also to the college of bishops in communion with the pope. Moreover, it is a gift of the entire Church as the biblical "pillar and ground of truth." Why should we be surprised, since Christ sent the Holy Spirit of truth on the Church at Pentecost?

The pontiff is as fallible in ordinary human matters as you and me. He can make mistakes of judgment just as we do. He can even make mistakes and have poor judgment in his personal theology and pastoral advice. Only when he makes a solemn pronouncement identifying the Church's doctrine in a particular belief is he preserved as the vicar of Christ from error. Infallibility is a protective charism, or grace, regarding the Church's faith: it is not a permission to invent new doctrines and ethics.

But Catholics believe in relics.

That all depends on what is meant by "believe in." Catholics use relics in much the same way anyone uses photos, keepsakes, and mementos of loved ones who have died. They are our only tangible contact now with those who were important in our lives. Catholics use them, too, because the relics are of not just any loved ones but of the Christian martyrs and saints.

Sometimes history attaches a miraculous healing power to a relic, but no Catholic is obliged to believe that this is a fact. (No Catholic is obliged to believe even in such rather spectacular occurrences as the miracles of Lourdes.) Our obligations of faith have to do with doctrine and ethics based in Scripture and sacred Tradition only. But some Catholics are like some people in any and all religions — they elevate an honorable devotion to a level of undue importance as if it were a requirement of faith.

Jesus exhorts us in the Bible, ". . . call no one your father on earth" (Matthew 23:9). So why do Catholics ignore the Bible in this?

The simplest answer here is to say that a totally prohibitionist interpretation (that of the Fundamentalists) conflicts with the fact that Jesus in other instances acknowledges human fatherhood and even makes complimentary references to it. For example, he commands us, "Honor your father and mother" (Mark 10:19). If the absolutist interpretation is correct, then Jesus here contradicts his own prohibition. But the absolutist meaning is incorrect.

In the context of "you are not to be called rabbi . . . call no one your father," Jesus is addressing the apostles (and ultimately Christian teachers). The contrast here is between Jesus as a true teacher who serves the apostles and the so-called great Jewish teachers whose relationship to their students was one of superiority. They loved the titles of "rabbi" (which means "my great one") and "father" (which demanded dependence).[5] "No one" thus refers to the rabbis, not to human or spiritual fatherhood in general. When Catholic, Orthodox, and Anglican congregations refer to their priests as fathers, they do so in the spiritual and pastoral sense only.

Catholic teaching on purgatory is an invention: it is not in the Bible.

The truth of that statement depends on whose version of the Bible one is using and whose authority stands behind that version. For Catholics, the Bible includes the Books of Maccabees. The Reformation tradition rejects them: the older Catholic (and the apostolic/early Church) tradition accepts them as inspired Scripture.

Second Maccabees 12:38-46 recounts the expiation for the Jewish troops who had died in battle but were found to have worn pagan amulets. Judas Maccabeus takes up a collection to be sent to the temple for an expiatory sacrifice, "taking account of the resurrection. For if he were not expecting that those who had fallen would rise again, it would have been superfluous and foolish to pray for the dead. But if he was looking to the splendid reward that is laid up for those who fall asleep in godliness, it was a holy and pious thought. Therefore he made atonement for the dead, so that they might be delivered from their sin."

Judas Maccabeus's theology sees not just two states — resurrection and obliteration (or heaven and hell) — in the afterlife but an intermediate state of purgation, or cleansing. Pastoral experience indicates that few people, even wonderful Christians, die in a perfect spiritual condition. Yet the Bible teaches that "nothing defiled shall go before the Lord" (see, for instance, Wisdom 7:25, Isaiah 25:8, and Habakkuk 1:13). No sinfulness, no matter how slight, can be allowed in heaven or be present in the eternal vision of God. Such would be a contradiction. For God is all-holy. Theology, trying to make sense of matters not clearly revealed, also suggests that there must be a temporary condition of cleansing after death for souls not ready for heaven nor worthy of hell. This is what the Church calls purgatory, a place of cleansing.

The great Fathers and Doctors of the Church as well as the inspirers of the divine liturgies of both East and West have written and preached on this state, or process, of purgation. Luther's "doctor of grace," St. Augustine, wrote: "There are some [believers] who have departed this life, not so bad as to be deemed unworthy of mercy, nor so good as to be entitled to immediate happiness" (*City of God*, xxi, 24). Where and how — if not in purgatory — are they to be purified?

This chapter does not address all the Catholic teachings that Fundamentalists (and others) claim are not Bible-based. Such a task would require not this chapter but a whole book. The reader is referred to Keating's *Catholicism and Fundamentalism*, a book that is listed in the endnotes of this chapter.

Many public libraries carry the *New Catholic Encyclopaedia* in their general reference sections. This multivolume work contains detailed articles on the questions discussed in this chapter and those in Keating's work. The reader might wish to consult it for that purpose, and for its general articles on the Bible: its formation, interpretation, and role in the Church. (*Our Sunday Visitor's Catholic Encyclopedia*, a one-volume work edited by Father

Peter Stravinskas, is also available, and can be ordered from your bookstore or by calling Our Sunday Visitor's toll-free number, 1-800-348-2440, and asking for an account representative.)

ENDNOTES

1. St. Augustine, *Epistolae*, 194, para. 19; quoted in Bertrand Conway, *The Question Box* (New York: Paulist Press-Deus Books, 1962), p. 45.
2. Karl Keating, *Catholicism and Fundamentalism* (San Francisco: Ignatius Press, 1988), p. 283.
3. St. Jerome, *Adversus Vigilius*, 6; quoted in Conway, op. cit., p. 282.
4. On infallibility, see Keating, op. cit., pp. 215-231.
5. See *A New Catholic Commentary on Holy Scripture*, ed. by R. C. Fuller (London: Nelson & Sons, 1969), p. 944.

TELL ME WHY I SHOULD BE A CATHOLIC WHEN...

what Catholics call sacraments seem like empty, ineffective rituals?

Many non-Catholics wonder why so much emphasis is placed on sacraments by Roman Catholics. They don't notice baptized Catholic children acting so different from other kids. Right after receiving Communion some Catholics go right back to gossiping, drinking, or conniving. Teenage Catholics seem just as wild as others even after confirmation. What is confession but a way to feel clean for a few hours only to sin again? Some say the divorce rate of Catholics is equal to that of non-Catholics — so marriage can't be that powerful a source of grace. Holy orders? Not so good a picture from the secular press, which doesn't have to cover up for scandals! Anointing of the sick? Comforting, no doubt, but you could go to a healing service by an anointed healer and get more "cures."

Others may not want to take such a skeptical approach about the effects of the sacraments but will question the scriptural justification for most if not all of the sacraments, at least as practiced in the Catholic Church.

One Catholic response to such questions is contained in my booklet *Signs of Love* (Boston: St. Paul Books and Media). This treatment is threefold: (1)

the scriptural basis for each sacrament; (2) reasons why Catholics consider the sacraments to be signs of Christ's love; and (3) explanations for why these great gifts are not always effective.

Brief answers to questions 1 and 2 will follow. Afterward a general section will address the issue of effectiveness.

As Catholics, we believe that Christ, the love of the Father made manifest, chose to come to us in intimate love through the sacraments. Love is never static. Love tends toward greater and greater intimacy of union. As the human lover continually strives to become closer and closer to the beloved, so the Divine Lover seeks means of entering deeply within us. Through the sacraments Christ comes to us concretely and visibly, though mysteriously: both visible and hidden. Is this not a material substance, and yet it manifests itself in visible signs — embraces, gifts. . . ?

Baptism

"Go therefore and make disciples of all nations, baptizing them in the name of the Father and of the Son and of the Holy Spirit" (Matthew 28:19).

Although every creature is born out of the loving hand of God, yet, because of original sin, we have lost spiritual participation in God's life. We are turned toward the pursuit of worldliness rather than toward God. But Christ's redemption has removed the barrier between us and God and opened the way to an essential reunion! We believe that Christ embraces his creatures in baptism and joins himself to them with a bond of love that can never be destroyed by him but only by us.

Thus, the purpose of baptism is not to provide us with a conscious religious experience but rather to open within us a door through which divine love can flow, to turn the soul toward God by implanting on it his first kiss, as it were.

To deny the child this expression of Christ's self-giving, on the grounds that the infant is too young to freely choose, would be similar to withholding parental love until the child is at the age of reason. Psychological studies show that tiny orphans have actually died when they were tended impersonally, so deeply did the lack of love affect them!

Given the infinite gulf between the reality of divine love and even the adult's ability to appreciate it, who shall set a time when the entering of Christ's love into the soul would have its greatest effect? In comparison with the love on God's part, we are always half asleep. Just as Christ has infinite love for this fresh individual, uniquely conceived, so the Church, manifesting the divine love, hastens to bring the infant into contact with her by making the child a member of the mystical body of the Church.

Holy Communion

" 'Take, eat; this is my body.' Then he took a cup, and after giving thanks, he gave it to them, saying, 'Drink from it, . . . for this is my blood of the covenant, which is poured out for many for the forgiveness of sins' " (Matthew 26:26-28).

Many say that Christ is to be found primarily in loving one's neighbor. They consider misspent the time taken to adore Christ in the Eucharist. To them, receiving Communion is less an immediate union with Christ than a symbol of Christ's desire to see his people gathered together at a communal meal.

True as it is that Christ wishes us to find him in the midst of human love, it is very clear that the truth of Christ's real presence in the Eucharist aims at a still more direct form of love.

Even in human love, we find a great desire to be actually in the presence of the beloved one. If someone would be willing to do anything for me but would shun my presence, I would feel hurt and unloved.

Being in the actual presence of someone I love causes a deep happiness, as tenderness heals the deep wounds of loneliness. Ultimately, when the love is strong enough, one longs for this person not only to be near but to become a part of one — in the intimate unity of marriage.

It appears, upon studying the gospels, that Christ wanted very much for us to experience his presence, to have us near him. He would gather his people "as a hen gathers her brood" (Luke 13:34). He lets the little children come to him. He permits the crowds to cluster around him. He even begs his friends to be present in his agony.

The deepest physical desire of lovers is actually to become one with each other, the physical act of intimacy being not only an ecstatic experience in itself but also, where it is the fruit of true love in marriage, a real union of hearts and spirits.

Jesus also wants to be absolutely one with us. He sees his beloved creatures wandering around aimlessly, inwardly locked up in their lonely egoism. Filled with compassion, he longs to enter into them, to comfort them, to let the leaven of his love lift up their spirits. Like a human lover, he cannot bear to see the ones he loves bowed down with melancholy, but instead he would give anything to be able to inject his own joy into their hearts.

Just as one kiss does not suffice for a lover, but he would come close to his loved one every day, so Christ offers himself to us in the intimacy of Communion every day, if we will. Each day we can live out of the unity of love, fed by the food of divine love, by the very being of Christ our Lover, who wants us to be part of him and, what is just as astounding, wants to be part of us.

Saints and mystics have experienced the truth of the real presence of Christ in the Eucharist in ecstasies not given to most Catholics. Frequently utilizing the analogy of romantic love, they have painted a vivid portrait of how Christ, like an unrequited lover, burns for the day when his beloved (each of us) will open to him so that he can pour his love into that soul, possess it, and, finally, bring it to perfect union with him in eternal bliss.

A very striking example of one who became a Catholic in spite of great doubts about our sacraments beforehand is Scott Hahn.

Scott Hahn was a Presbyterian minister, married with three children. As a seminarian he was known for his hatred for the Catholic Church, which he considered to be the personification of the devil — the anti-Christ to come as portrayed in the New Testament.

In the course of his Protestant studies he began to find that contrary to all expectation, many times it was the Catholic Church that held to truths he wanted to emphasize himself as a minister of God's word. As he describes it, his ardent interest in finding where Christian truth was believed and lived became first a detective story, then a horror story when he found more and more of this truth in the Church he had regarded as hellish, and finally a romance. By the end of his long journey he was fairly panting for the Eucharist he had previously so scorned.

Scott Hahn and his wife, who afterward also came into the full communion of the Catholic faith, are now ministering at the Franciscan University of Steubenville in their program of teaching Catholics how to evangelize.

It would be counterproductive to summarize Hahn's manner of defending the sacraments. Thousands of Protestants and also Catholics are enjoying his fine tapes covering the sacraments and every other topic that alienates Protestants from the Catholic Church — taught from the point of view of a former Protestant minister in a tremendously dynamic, convincing manner. (These and other tapes under the title of *Answering Common Objections* by Scott Hahn are readily available.)

Ross Porter is another witness coming from a Protestant church background. Ross was studying to be a Presbyterian minister and Christian psychologist when he discovered that more and more he agreed with Catholic rather than Protestant theological positions. Easter of 1992 was when he was brought into full communion in the Catholic Church. Here is what Ross Porter says about the Eucharist, which seems to him, as a psychologist, such an important source of wholeness as it reaches into the soul through the body's reception:

"Give us this day our daily bread" ... the Eucharist is so full of meaning and power that words and concepts could never fully define it. The Eucharist makes explicit the Life of the Body. The Risen Lord offering Himself to me, and integrating the splintered parts of my being: mind, body, spirit. Who am I? "You are a new creation." Where am I going? "Take, eat, this is my body."

The Body and Blood of my Savior reminds me of my true identity, and my eternal destination. Images flood my mind: the Sacred Heart, bursting for love; the Unblemished Lamb sacrificed for love; the New and Everlasting Covenant, Incarnated for love. The Word became flesh, and what God has brought together, let no one put asunder. Christ the High Priest, communicating His grace to me; tears of thanksgiving flow as I experience His healing touch. He wants to give Himself to me, completely. It is more than I can grasp; much more than I deserve. "Come unto me you who are heavy laden and I will give you rest." The Eucharist is rest; it is a safe haven, a refuge. A Priceless Gift offered for free. "Blessed are those who hunger and thirst for righteousness, for they will be filled."

TELL ME WHY I SHOULD BE A CATHOLIC WHEN...

'they' have changed the Church so much?

The Second Vatican Council was a gathering of the pope and bishops of the Church in the early 1960s — from October 1962 to December 1965, to be exact. Its purpose was to address issues and topics regarded as pastorally necessary in our time. The Church desired, among other things, to open a dialogue with other religions as well as the world at large. The Church desired to put herself at the service of humankind's great aspirations and needs, to encourage and inspire men and women to universal goodness, to support justice and peace everywhere, to help eliminate war and famine and poverty. Internally, the Church through the council wished to renew herself spiritually and to seek holiness as never before. A renewal of faith, of liturgical life, of a more biblically based morality and teaching was called for. Such a vast renewal and profound vision was bound to become a huge (and often disturbing) challenge to the pastors and people of the Church.

Many Catholics became disoriented. We began to hear some complain that "they" have changed the Church too much. Others felt "they" had not changed the Church sufficiently. The practical implementation of the Second Vatican Council's sixteen documents was not easy. We remember Pope Paul VI complaining of "misguided" and even "false" interpretations of the renewal called for by the council. To this day, one can meet in our parishes Catholics who strongly believe that the Church has been so decisively changed that she is no longer the Catholic Church. We disagree with them. Yes, there have been changes — changes in emphases and in directions, but there is no change in any of the essentials by which the Church defines herself — doctrine, morals, and grace.

One lesson we have all learned from the reactions to Vatican Council II is how much people confuse the nonessential with the essential, and how much the external dress of Catholicism (or of any institution) is confused with its substance. And yet in the world of everyday life we would never dream of confusing the packaging with the package, the wrappings and ribbons with the gift itself. People argued over the Mass in Latin versus the Mass in the vernacular and forgot that the Mass remained. People continue to bicker over new rules for receiving the sacraments when the real issue is proper preparation for the reception and celebration of the same unchanging sacraments. People argue over catechism and religious education as if the doctrines of the Catholic faith had changed (they have not) when what has changed is the way the doctrines are presented according to contemporary methods of teaching.

However, one may admit that "the changes" were poorly explained to the people from the very start. And one may also admit that there were people in the Church (as there are now) pushing their own agenda, pushing their interpretation of how liturgy should be conducted and how catechism should be taught. And it is these items (not core faith and salvation) that have so distracted and distressed priests and people in our time. What a senseless waste of energy, mission, and direction! Because so much is being conducted in daily pastoral life from such sources and bases, the ordinary priest and parishioner should be comforted in knowing that it is okay to challenge these, for we are dealing here not with the authority of the council but with opinions that ought to be subjected to scrutiny and validation.

Let us look at some items that disturb the average parish today. The option of receiving Holy Communion in the hand or on the tongue is not an expression of irreverence for the Lord but an expression of the fact that he can be approached as the majestic God or as St. Paul called him, "our Brother." We can take in hand, if we so wish, the august Lord who said "Take and eat" as he broke the bread and gave it to the apostles who took it in their hands. Why do people make such an issue of this when the real issue is our faith and gratitude for "so wondrous a sacrament"?

Similarly, if the Church has decided that the issue of priestly ordination of women is not a question to be resolved by popular demand but by theological investigation into whether or not the Church has the competency to ordain women, why do so many of us react viscerally on one side or the other of the question?

If the official legislation on liturgical rule and/or option tells us that the tabernacle may be retained behind the altar (but emptied of the Blessed Sacrament during a celebration of Mass) or relocated in a special chapel, why do we in the United States so frequently insist on the second option only? If the general liturgical principles instruct us to place the presider's chair behind the altar or elevated to the side, why do some liturgical commissions insist on placing it in front of the altar? And if our culture (which the Vatican Council says must be respected) has us sit in pews, why are some American liturgists trying to impose a basically "stand only" practice on us during Mass?

None of these aberrations come from the Second Vatican Council — they come from the new imperialism of individuals with influence, unfortunately, in many dioceses and parishes. But these are precisely the nonessential issues that upset many people. No one seems to want to face the issue of the right of the flock not to be subjected to continual aggravation. These are the issues, too, that contribute to the nonacceptance of Vatican II and the authority of the bishops.

Most divisive of all, perhaps, is the area of catechetics. Here we have honest efforts at new teaching methods ruined by lack of content and, consequently, reduced to mere grounds for battle. We have reactionaries who want nothing but content transmitted and liberals who understand the catechetical enterprise as "fun and games." We have "trained" catechists with master's degrees who lack knowledge of Catholic teachings and others with master's degrees (and without them) who are highly proficient in Catholic doctrine. We have catechists and parish directors of religious education who seem to despise doctrine, who insist that their role is to give children "happy memories" only. We have others who seem to operate from a philosophy of cramming as much doctrine as possible into the child's head. Clearly, there is room for fun and doctrine, for content and a happy process, for learning and for happy memories. Why do we lack balance in so many diocesan departments and parishes in these matters? Why are not more of the doctrinally balanced and self-integrated people operating these programs? Please do not blame Vatican II or a "changed" Church. Neither is at fault. Poor local Church judgment (diocesan and parochial) is.

It is the areas of liturgy and catechesis that most involve the ordinary believer. He or she should not be at all afraid to question or challenge issues of methodology and content in the religious instruction of children, since parents, according to Vatican Council II, are the primary religious educators of their children.[1] Dioceses have a process for the adjudication of disputes. Similarly, parishioners may challenge various liturgical innovations and Church "renovations" that (over the years) have sometimes proven themselves to be unwarranted interpretations of the liturgical renewal. Tabernacles have been removed from behind the altar on the misinformation that such is required by the general principles of the liturgy. Other changes occur based on directions and guidelines that are improperly elevated to the stature of liturgical law. And some liturgical impositions have no more authority than the whim of some "expert." Liturgy and catechetics are vitally the concern of the believer, yet it is all too often the experience of believers that they find little relief and a lot of dogmatism from those who should serve them in these crucial areas of their life and concern. Recourse is possible. Our Catholic people should not be timid about demanding their rights in the local diocese and parish.

Yet we must concentrate on the essentials of faith and practice. Nothing essential has changed in doctrine, sacraments, or morals. At least nothing has changed in these areas with the Church or because of Vatican Council II. But some people within the Church claim false changes in the name of the council and others live secularized lives. But it is neither the Church nor the council that has changed them; it is their own surrender to the secular humanism of our pagan culture and society.

Some of the genuine changes that have happened as a result of the Second Vatican Council are good but challenging to all of us. We are asked to pay greater attention to the Scriptures. We are asked to be more ecumenical and outreaching to other Christians and other believers. We are asked to take more personal responsibility for penance and fasting. We are asked to celebrate more often the true social and community nature of our beautiful faith by emphasizing the community of believers when we exchange the sign of peace at Mass or conduct part of the sacrament of reconciliation together prior to individual confession and absolution. Nothing is wrong with this. On the contrary, it is appropriate — because we are the Church, the body of the Lord, the community of faith, the fellowship of love. Religion has a horizontal as well as a vertical dimension: we love God *and* our neighbor for love of him. Vatican II has merely called us to this kind of renewal or direction, to this kind of concern and love that became somewhat lost in the silence and sterility of recent generations. In many ways, the Church has merely returned to old ways and older habits of the heart.

The Church is directed infallibly and unfailingly by the Holy Spirit given to her that Pentecost morning. Already, that Spirit has illuminated her through twenty councils. There will be others between now and when the Lord comes again in glory. Why, then, are we so fearful? Why do we lack confidence in the Spirit of truth? Are we really afraid that the Church has changed in essentials or is it that we are afraid to follow the Spirit of truth and change ourselves and our too comfortable familiarities? Let the Spirit answer for each of us.

Another way we know that "they" have not changed the Church is from the fact that Fundamentalists still bring the same prejudices and objections against the Church as they did before Vatican Council II was convened. Not an iota has changed! They see no change in our Mass, in our sacraments, in the priesthood, in our moral and ethical teachings. The anti-Catholic graffiti that appear on some of our parish churches are identical (word for word) with the same theological graffiti that appeared before the council. The questions we train our seminarians to respond to in pastoral apologetics class today are the ones we were trained in over thirty years ago — before the Second Vatican Council.

Protestant ministers join the Church today as they did in the past — for the very teachings and sacraments that have not changed in their substance, meaning, and grace. What brought the Cardinal Newmans and the Monsignor Knoxes and the Father Fabers into the Church in past generations still brings in the Scott Hahns and the Richard Neuhauses and the Dr. Johns today.

The reception of a man like Malcolm Muggeridge into the Catholic Church is a good example of how nothing of substance has changed in the Church when scrutinized against the backdrop of her history by such a pungent critic. He is a witness to embracing the Catholic Church in spite of changes one might deem to be unfortunate.

Muggeridge was born in 1903 into a socialistic English family. Up until age seventy he scoffed at Christian beliefs. During this time he was a journalist, wartime spy for Britain, and TV talk-show personality. He was known for his wit, sarcasm, and cynicism. But all of this changed when he met Mother Teresa during the filming of a program on her work with the poor. His book *Something Beautiful for God* describes the enormous impact made on this worldly man by becoming acquainted with a holy woman. When Muggeridge began to go public with his newfound Christian faith he was dubbed St. Mugg by his still-atheistic friends in the world of media and journalism.

Evangelical Christians hailed him as one of their own, but Roman Catholics were praying for his entrance into our Church. On his numerous speaking tours, he was often asked whether he had yet become a Catholic. To this he would reply that he still lacked the grace, but also he was troubled by the way the Church was being harmed by dissent and laxity within. He wanted to join the solemn, noble Church of the saints of old as opposed to a broken-down ruin of a church. Nonetheless, his need for the essentials, especially for a church that could endure the evil of the world as well as its own troubles, and God's grace (no doubt assisted by the encouragement of Mother Teresa) finally broke down all his resistance.

A few years before his death in 1990, Muggeridge and his wife did become Catholics. He wrote: "The Catholic Church has a special niche today for 20th century lost souls who, in the empty caverns they inhabit, take comfort from the enclosing sounds of sanctus bells, and benedictions, and absolutions. . . ."[2] It is said that he faced his approaching death without the slightest fear.

ENDNOTES

1. See "Declaration on Christian Education" (Nos. 3, 7, 8) and "Pastoral Constitution on the Church in the Modern World" (No. 48), *Vatican Council II* (Collegeville, Minn.: Liturgical Press, 1984).
2. Information taken from George Mitrovich, "The Death of St. Mugg" in *Christian Century*, Vol. 107, Nov. 21-28, 1990 (pp. 1085-1086).

TELL ME WHY I SHOULD BE A CATHOLIC WHEN...

women are second-class citizens in the Church?

Many women both outside and inside the Church wonder about the position of the female gender in Church history and also in the present day. Given the growing equality of women in society it can seem as if the Roman Catholic Church is really backward and even unjust in the roles from which women are excluded and also in noninclusive use of language.

Some women (as well as some men) ask: Since God is so tender and merciful, why isn't God referred to as our Mother as well as our Father? Why are there so many references to man, brothers, and brethren in Scripture, liturgy, and song in the Catholic Church and so few to woman, sisters, or persons (including both women and men)? Since nowadays there are female presidents of countries, women doctors, female soldiers, women rabbis, and female Protestant ministers, why should the priesthood be excluded from women in the Catholic Church? After all, there seem to be no direct statements of Jesus in the Bible against having women in the priesthood! Isn't it especially distressing when you have many priests concelebrating a Mass and no women with them? Should educated women with degrees have to get permission from a priest for everything they want to do? Isn't that treating grown women like little girls? Patronizing!

Could it be that male-dominated societies in biblical times excluded women from leadership in order to hog the power themselves? If these discriminatory attitudes still persist for psychological and sociological reasons, isn't it due time either to reverse this in the Church today or to shun any religious group, especially the Catholic Church, that treats women as second-class citizens?

Let us look at the issue of inclusive language first. What inclusive language means is language that reflects the fact that persons come in both sexes. For example: speaking about a mixed group of male and female human beings as persons is inclusive. The opposite — exclusive language — occurs when both sexes are designated with a masculine word such as "man" or "he."

Such exclusive language can often be found in ordinary speech, in literature, in Scripture, and in worship. Even if in the past people meant the word "man" or "he" to refer to both sexes, and women understood that they were also included in some cases (not on the doors of bathrooms!), many feminists in our day insist that the use of "man" in instances where both women and men are meant is anti-feminine.

Why? Because it makes it seem as if the male sex is the model and the female sex secondary. If the only purpose of using "man" to include both sexes were to save time and paper then we could use "woman" to include both men and women, but we never do. Using "exclusive" male-oriented language is therefore thought to reflect what is called a "patriarchal culture," that is, one in which men dominate over women.

It is important to explain further the difference between what is called horizontal and vertical exclusive language. Horizontal language refers to human persons such as talking about "man, men, he, brothers," or "you guys," when women are also being talked about. Inclusive-language advocates want to see such words replaced by person, humankind, women and men, children of God, brothers and sisters.

Vertical language refers to the concept of God as masculine, as in Father, or he, or Lord. Inclusive-language advocates want to see such designations replaced by God the Creator or the Holy Spirit, or even she. In referring to God's ways, such feminists wish to see more mention of traditionally feminine traits as pertaining to God, as in "She is tender and merciful."

Whether it be horizontal or vertical language in question, the hope is that changing words to be more inclusive will be educative. Women will feel more included, will believe that their dignity is being honored, and both men and women will gradually understand that feminine aspects of God (for example, empathy) are equally important as masculine elements (for instance, power). Hopefully, changes in language will also reflect and lead to better relationships between men and women in family life, the workplace, and in the Church.

A related question involves use of words by men in society and in the Church that reflect a belittling of women such as calling a grown woman "the girl," as in "Tell the girl to bring my coffee in now" in an office situation.

Challenged especially by feminists within the

Church, there have been recent endeavors to address exclusive-language issues. In 1990 the National Conference of Catholic Bishops issued a statement called "Criteria for the Evaluation of Inclusive Language Translations."

In this document the bishops make a clear distinction between horizontal and vertical language. Acknowledging the changes in perception that make referring to women and men together with words like "man" or "he" or "brothers" they recommend the use instead of inclusive words such as person, people, and human family. They note that in the original languages of the Bible and liturgical texts collective words meant human beings in general.

"The Word of God proclaimed to all nations is by nature inclusive, that is, addressed to all peoples, women and men. Consequently, every effort should be made to render the language of biblical translations as inclusively as a faithful translation of the text permits, especially when this concerns the People of God, Israel, and the Christian community" (No. 14).

Instances where changes would not be justified include prophetic passages where the use of "he" refers ultimately to a male person such as Jesus or "she" for a female person such as Mary, interpreted as referred to by words such as "the woman."

The meaning of language does change in the course of history. For example, a word like "Negro," originally thought of by many as neutral, is now experienced by Afro-Americans as conveying a sense of inferiority because of its associations with slavery. Charity invites us not to use the word "Negro" any more.

Charitable patience would also come into the picture when women restrain themselves from jumping on men who are used to speaking of women as girls. Gentle humor might make the point better than attributing motives of scorn to men who have just never thought about it deeply.

With respect to vertical language about God, the bishops take a different stance:

> Great care should be taken in translations of the names of God and in the use of pronouns referring to God. While it would be inappropriate to attribute gender to God as such, the revealed Word of God consistently uses a masculine reference for God. It may sometimes be useful, however, to repeat the name of God, as used earlier in the text, rather than use the masculine pronoun in every case. But care must be taken that the repetition not become tiresome.
>
> The classic translation of the Tetragrammaton (YHWH) as Lord and the translation of Kyrios as Lord should be used in lectionaries.
>
> Feminine imagery in the original language of the biblical texts should not be obscured or replaced by the use of masculine imagery in English translations, e.g., Wisdom literature.
>
> Christ is the center and focus of all Scripture. The New Testament has interpreted certain texts of the Old Testament in an explicitly Christological fashion (that is, as referring to the future Messiah). Special care should be observed in the translation of these texts so that the Christological meaning is not lost. . . .
>
> In fidelity to the inspired Word of God, the traditional biblical usage for naming the Persons of the

Trinity as Father, Son, and Holy Spirit is to be retained. Similarly, in keeping with New Testament usage and the Church's tradition, the feminine pronoun is not to be used to refer to the Person of the Holy Spirit.

In relation to vertical language, John Paul II points out often that, since Jesus calls God his Father, his choice of wording is normative for us.

"But why did Jesus refer to God as Father?" you might still ask. "Isn't this just because he lived in a patriarchal society?" To think that in such important matters Jesus was simply programmed by his times is to demean his divine nature and God's providence. God could have become incarnate as a female in a matriarchal society. In this case a female Messiah might have called God "Mother." As believers in a religion not made up by us to express spiritual yearnings but revealed by God, it is important to trust that if God reveals himself as Father, we must ponder that choice rather then reverse it.

Suggestions have been made to avoid the problem of male/female altogether by referring to God as "it" or as Creator rather than as Father or Mother. Such neutral words, however, run the risk of altering the Christian religion to the point of being more philosophical and abstract than being personal and concrete. The word "Father" is full of human meaning for all peoples, whereas Creator is a vaguer and colder word.

For more about vertical language about God, see John Paul II's apostolic letter "On the Dignity and Vocation of Woman," and Donald Bloesch's *The Battle for the Trinity*.

To turn now to the even more controversial issue of the ordination of women, the Church has always interpreted the choice of Jesus to have only male apostles in spite of the preeminent holiness of his Mother, Mary, as indicating that he wished to ordain only men to the office of the priesthood. (On the testimony of the tradition see "Declaration on the Question of the Admission of Women to the Ministerial Priesthood" by the Sacred Congregation for the Doctrine of the Faith, 1976.)

Since Jesus was countercultural in his attitudes toward women, calling them to discipleship on an equal basis with men and breaking down many traditional Jewish barriers between men and women, it is misleading to think that the Lord was simply following customs of discrimination in his choice of males as apostles.

But isn't it discriminatory toward women to have only male priests? Not really. Scripture teaches that equality of personhood can be affirmed even though God-given roles are different. Even in the Trinity the Son is different from the Father, but that doesn't mean that he is an inferior "second-class citizen"!

A woman was chosen for the highest honor of all those of the human race: Mary, the Mother of God. Men do not resent this choice as discriminatory, as if that made Joseph a second-class citizen.

God has a right to create differences between the sexes, which are not in opposition but complementary in character. In a good Catholic parish the pastor and his associates will take counsel with women of prayer and express their gratitude often for the many gifts women bring to the life of the community. Some observers of the Church scene today say Catholic women have more ministries than Protestant women; moreover, that power is really with the bishop rather than the parish priest.

Yet women still wonder: "Don't we need both women and men to image Christ at the altar?" The answer is that it was God's own will that his incarnate form be masculine. Jesus was the Son of God, not the daughter. Jesus came proclaiming himself as the bridegroom, a male image, with the Church as his bride (see, for instance, Mark 2:19-20, John 3:29, and Revelation 19:7).

Unlike some other Christian churches that give little weight to symbolism, it is part of the God-willed tradition of the Catholic Church to use physical symbols to express invisible spiritual realities. St. Thomas Aquinas taught that "sacramental signs represent what they signify by natural resemblance." Just as Christ chose the material elements of bread and wine rather than crackers and soda to become transubstantiated by his grace into his own body and blood, the apt symbol of the Person of Christ who says in the words of Consecration, "This is my body, this is my blood," is a priest who images Christ as the Son rather than as the daughter of God.

This does not mean that women have no strong leadership roles in the Church. The example of Mary and the women saints points to the extremely crucial role women play in God's plan. After all, who do we remember, St. Catherine of Siena or her parish priest?

What is more, in recent times more and more leadership roles have been opened to women such as financial head of a diocese or parish administrator, not to mention the age-old influence of sisters in school and hospital administration.

For more information on the question of ordaining women see Manfred Hauke's exhaustive book *Women in the Priesthood?* translated by David Kipp (San Francisco: Ignatius Press, 1988).

Are there women who are strong on feminist issues but who agree with the Church's teachings?

Yes. Many. An interesting example from the first half of this century was Edith Stein. A German philosophy student, Edith espoused the feminist cause. Although considering traditional motherly roles to be beautiful, she also explained why women need to be encouraged in their other talents. When she became a Catholic, she wanted to be a Carmelite nun and this role did not make her feel second-class at all. Her lectures and writings on women have become very influential, especially since her beatification.

An American writer of great ability and perceptiveness, Juli Loesch Wiley was originally a Catholic feminist involved with groups who were interested in liturgical innovations aimed at acquainting Catholics with the goodness of referring to God as Mother and the need for women in the priesthood. Now a Feminist for Life, she writes numerous articles about why it is better for the priesthood to be masculine. She believes that Jesus chose men only to be priests so that his message that tender spiritual love was more important than power, lust, or wealth would be conveyed by transformed Christian male leaders, who need that message the most!

A Catholic theologian, Mary Neill, O.P., co-author with me of *A Woman's Tale*, thinks that because it is of woman's body that we come and survive from womb and breast-milk, we need males to give us our supernatural body and blood in the Mass — for balance!

In my book *Feminine, Free and Faithful* I explain why a woman is stronger and freer, as were the female saints, when rather than insisting on priestly roles, we follow the Holy Spirit to come into spiritual authority.

Conclusion

We fervently hope that *Tell Me Why* has at least made you more interested in exploring the Catholic Church in greater depth.

If so, here are some suggestions:

❦ Say a daily prayer summing up the stage you have reached in your quest. (An atheist might pray: "God, if there is a God, show me where to find you!" A non-Catholic presently part of another religion might pray: "Spirit of God, if there is a fullness of truth and grace I am not now receiving, please show me where." A former Catholic might pray: "Jesus, remove any prejudices I may have that come from unhappy experiences of the past, and if you want me back in the Catholic Church, let me have the faith to make contact with my parish or some other source of further guidance.")

❦ Visit a Catholic bookstore or library and seek out pamphlets and books about topics only discussed briefly in this one. (You can also contact Our Sunday Visitor and ask about what is available on topics of the Catholic faith you are interested in learning more about: call toll-free, 1-800-348-2440, and ask for an account representative; or write Our Sunday Visitor, Attn: Book and Pamphlet Sales, 200 Noll Plaza, Huntington, IN 46750.)

❦ Call up the nearest Catholic Church and find out the schedule of liturgies or other services and visit — or ask to speak to the pastor.